TERRY LOVELETTE

Thoughts from a Walk

GREEN MOUNTAIN MUSINGS

Chapin Keith Publishing
Daleville, VA. 24083
www.chapinkeith.com

Publisher's Cataloging-in-Publication Data

Names: Lovelette, Terry - author.
Title: Thoughts from a Walk / Terry Lovelette

Identifiers: LCCN: 2023919475 | ISBN: 9781734480795 (Hardcover) |
9781734480788 (Paperback) | 978-1-7344907-6-4 (eBook)
BISAC POETRY / General | POETRY/ American/General | NATURE/ Essays

Cover and book design by Asya Blue Design

All photos including the cover are by Terry Lovelette except as noted

First Edition

This book is dedicated to kind souls everywhere. Continue to walk your path and shine your light. The world needs you!

Contents

Introduction

I grew up in the small northwestern Vermont mill town called Sheldon Springs. It was a great place to live. We had room to roam in the woods and the freedom to do so. With a close group of friends, we explored the cow paths and native trails in the surrounding woodlands. Climbing rocky hills, swimming in local watering holes, hiking through the woods, and sleeping under the stars. It's the place where I developed a connection with nature and a love for my home state of Vermont. From that connection, a bond of loyalty was established along with a deep appreciation for the forest settings and mountainous terrain that exists right here in my own backyard.

Although, as it often goes in life, age and responsibilities pulled me in other directions. Making my way in a career, raising children, and attending to community interests became the path. Mountain time took its place as a luxury item. I suppose there is no fault in that way. In some respects, it's called normal, and it filled my days.

But there is a quiet light that shines in every heart. It calls no attention to itself, yet it always shines. Illuminating the way and offering glimpses of beauty, serenity, and peace. Over the last 15 years I rediscovered this internal light by walking through the mountains of Vermont. As one of my favorite authors, John O'Donohue, alluded to in his book *Eternal Echoes*: "There are no manuals that provide directions on how to construct the individual you would like to become. Only you can decide this and only you can commit to taking up the lifetime of work that it demands." (1) To some the task is too daunting and retreat becomes the driving force. But for those with the fortitude to journey on, a wonderful privilege is offered. One that is framed in Grace and warmly presents itself to anyone who is willing to go to any length to find their way through the maze of possibilities that exist. While not always easy, it's an exciting adventure to grow into the person that your deepest longing desires intuitively lead you to be. It is also a great blessing.

With continued inspiration from John O'Donohue, I've come to realize that finding a creative harmony between my soul and life is to discover a precious gift. It's indeed true that there isn't much that I can do about the major problems of the world. Likewise, I am unable to change the way anyone else chooses to live their life. But by waking up to the eternal beauty and light of my own soul I am better equipped to accept life on life's terms. That acceptance offers me an opportunity to engage in life with a new set of lenses. With that improved vision the internal light of everything glows a little brighter, and shines rays of hope. This gift of life freely presents itself to me as I walk along mountain trails. My belief is that the enlightenment of a mountain experience is given to us for ourselves and also to bring peace, courage, and compassion to others.

I make an attempt in this book to share nature's insight in words. But expressing the depth of a mountain experience in writing always seems to come up short. I can offer a perspective and provide a description, but I can't bring the elements that touch you through your senses into prose. If you have experienced the sensation of the effects that the elements have on oneself, then perhaps you can relate. Otherwise, perhaps you can imagine. Regardless, the reason that I enjoy long walks in the mountains and prolonged stays in the backcountry, is so that I can become uncomfortable. For me it's become more than a mission to plant my flag on a summit or to check off a list of achievements. Not that there is anything wrong with that approach. Many of my hikes have been fueled by a desire to reach a goal. However, at the age of 65, most often I hike and climb to embrace the challenges, to become inspired, to experience the sensations, to enjoy the air, to absorb the views, firsthand, raw, and real. These experiences help me feel fully alive and enable me to learn more about myself, as well as the world around me. The process of hiking and climbing helps me see the world from a unique perspective. One where I am small and insignificant. Through the mountains, I become right sized and humbled. I also appreciate the significance of being present in the moment. Like the mountains, I exist. I can conjure up all kinds of meaningful metaphors to help explain that existence. But at this time in my life, I can simply say that being in the mountains helps me understand my purpose.

To some, the mountains have no meaning. To me, they are meaningful. As I vibrate with life, so do the mountains and all that they cradle in their silence. That shared vibration brings insight, relevance, and understanding to anyone who allows themselves to listen. I have an appreciation for this truth not in my mind, but in my heart. This revelation opens a gateway to the soul and allows space for the seeds of growth to germinate and prosper. I understand how meaningless it is to try to capture what cannot be expressed in words. Yet, I'm compelled to write.

In the quiet solitude of the Green Mountains, I let all of this soak in. For me, the beauty of the many serene settings just off the beaten trail of rural Vermont bring a purposeful meaning to my life. I also realize that it doesn't come for free. The Long Trail system has been a fixture in Vermont for well over one hundred years. Under the artful management of the Green Mountain Club, this eternal golden braid has continued to weave its way along the spine of the Green Mountains. It was created long before I arrived, and it will continue to exist long after I'm gone. I owe a debt of gratitude to all the hardy souls who have labored to build, maintain, adapt, and grow one of Vermont's most vital resources.

Thus, my partner Sherry King and I are lifetime members of the GMC. We also do what we can to make continued financial contributions to help fund the Club's ongoing efforts. For us, donating to the GMC is a token of appreciation and gratitude for the joy that we get to experience in the Green Mountains of Vermont. It helps us feel more connected to the beauty of our home State. We also know what it's like to walk along the many ridge lines of the mountain range. From following the white blazes from Massachusetts to the Canadian border, to winding along a blue blazed side trail, the efforts of the GMC are ever present. It's the least we can do to contribute to their work. Many thanks to the GMC for the mountain of work that you climb. You bring deep meaning to the mountain experiences in Vermont.

From my end, I offer this book with deep humility. Well aware that my voice is just one voice of many. My only hope is that you find meaning in these words and that they help inspire you to enjoy your own journey to the fullest extent possible. All the best to you as you make your way. We live in a beautiful place...

A Perspective

Several hundred million years ago what is now Vermont collided with a western moving land mass that contained the rest of the northeast. According to geological records, the collision caused a buckling of the land where the future Green Mountain State would exist. Mountains formed in the process, and they would be further sculpted by, volcanoes, glacial forces, water, tectonic shifts, animals, and humans over the course of time. Collectively, these elements would conspire to craft the landscape that we get to experience today. Quite an amazing reality when you take a moment to consider it all.

In my opinion, these realities offer a perspective that can serve as a grounding force for those of us making our way within the human condition. All of us are here on this earth for a very brief moment in time. A tiny blip in the cosmic flow. With all the diversity that makes up the human race, the fact that each of us come with an expiration date is the one common denominator that we all share. Not to sound fatalistic, but this truism is one that I keep in the forefront of my mind. Frankly, if today is my last day, I don't want to leave as a resentful or bitter man. A simple philosophy for this simple soul.

Instead, I do my level best to appreciate my life and each person that's in it, even folks that I might not always see eye to eye with. Many good books offer direction on how to go about incorporating this principle (and others) into your life. Really, it's just good orderly direction that has been handed down for eons. Nothing too exotic, it requires a simple awareness and a willingness to engage in a practice of introspection.

An appreciation of these principles also helps me embrace the beautiful place that I get to live in. The quaint little Green Mountain State, the magnificent country called The United States of America, and the mysterious little blue ball flying through the universe that we all call Earth.

About 2500 years ago (as claimed by Epictetus, Golden Sayings, XV) Socrates said the following: "I am not an Athenian or a Greek but a citizen of the world." (2) I pay my respects today by struggling to make those words my own. Sometimes that means that I have to listen twice as much as I speak, then unlearn things that I think I know, so that I can remain open to learning a deeper truth. I have a lot more to learn but I'm making some progress.

Clarity

I spent a couple of days hiking in the nearby White Mountains of New Hampshire with my friend, Nate, and his trusty canine companion, Nali the wonder dog. Day one we climbed Mount Osceola and Day two we trekked across the Tripyramids. It was an enjoyable time.

For me, and seemingly for Nate and Nali, hiking and climbing is more than a mission to check off a summit. There is a deeper meaning to it all that brings with it some clarity. The least of which is the realization of just how small and insignificant I am. Along with that realization comes an acceptance of the fact that there is a significance hidden within each of us working our way through the human condition. True even for the soul of Nali and the friendly black bear that we encountered along the way. We are all embraced within creation. Walking my way through the backcountry comes with an ample amount of silence. Within the silence rests a breeding ground for contemplative thought. Within the contemplation is where the clarity exists.

While not a choice that everyone makes, I choose to make prayer and meditation a daily part of my life. That practice has been beneficial for me, and it provides me with solid direction. Regardless of where I am, the option to call on my practice is a reliable tool. Sometimes I forget this truth and there's nothing like a long walk in the mountains to help me sort it all out. Each step forward gets me farther away from the din of society and the chaotic impulses that come with it. In my opinion, we waste a lot of time engaged in meaningless things. I am not pointing fingers because I do it too. From my perspective these impulses are part of an egocentric world brought on by the human condition that we all live in.

Perhaps Thomas Keating said it best in some of his work on the human condition. I can see the logic in his suggestions that point toward the necessity of growing up; psychologically, spiritually, and emotionally. Within the process of maturing comes more clarity and a vision of what it means to be of service.

The mountains just lay there cloaked by a perennial philosophy. Patiently waiting for a passerby to listen for the silence where the eternal wisdom lies.

Distractions

Sometimes, the best choice for me is to eat a ham and cheese sandwich from a rocky perch. I like Laraway Mountain in particular. It is close to home, normally quiet on a weekday, and has a soothing panoramic view. The drive to the trailhead is enjoyable, and the trail itself has a diverse terrain that I find interesting.

The climb up serves the purpose of working me enough so that I get outside of my comfort zone. Worldly distractions, brought on by too much "screen time" subside, and once I find my pace for the day, I have an opportunity to walk in quiet contemplation. In so doing, I get to appreciate the present moments.

In the mountains, it becomes apparent quickly that there are a lot of things bigger than me. This realization helps keep me rightsized and more closely aligned with a power which is much greater than myself. Call it what you will. Debate over a definition isn't important to me. Instead, my focus centers on the reality that it helps me sort out what's relevant in life as I bumble along within the human condition.

Each day is a gift, and at the center of that day, there is a special place for my faith, my family, my friends, and life in general. A place that provides a source of intention along with a measure of equanimity. Even on an overcast day, the lookout offers a commanding view along with an opportunity for some introspective thought.

As it is in my life, I have nothing perfected, and I sometimes chew on things a little longer than I should. In fact, distractions and my path in life go hand in hand. Without fail, these distractions are my best teacher.

Like good teachers, distractions test my mettle, offer a glimpse of humility, and bring on conditions that shake me up a bit. Just enough most days to keep me awake.

Frankly, it's a little shocking sometimes to see just how far out of it we can be so much of the time. In the middle of the rat race there are many opportunities to latch on to distractions that provide an avenue to vent our annoyances, frustrations, resentments, and many other willy-nilly thoughts that arise. Within those distractions, along with the subsequent pissing and moaning, there are many lessons that spur us forward.

I don't know what it's like to be anyone else. But I can attest to the fact that I'm becoming more familiar with what it's like to me. Like my climb up the mountain, I make a little progress each day and one step at a time. As the moments of my day ensue, I have a chance of learning more about what lies within my distractions and comprehend the forces that might be working below the surface.

I have nothing perfected. Instead, inch by inch and day by day, I make a little more progress. I am eternally grateful for that Grace that rests within the boundless source of love which spurs me on. I welcome the nudging's that come through my distractions and appreciate the wake-up calls. They help keep me present and more aware of where my feet are. Thankfully, today, my feet led me here...We live in a beautiful place!

In Memory of Henry David

With great reverence, Henry David Thoreau wrote about nature at a level that was deep and thought provoking. Over the course of time, his writings have encouraged countless souls to engage in and appreciate Nature. As he alluded to, Nature isn't something we have, it's something that we are. It can be felt in every sunrise and appreciated within the serenity of the setting sun. All that is required from us is to pick up our heads, listen, look around, and appreciate what we see. Thankfully, most days I do.

However, I still spend a lot of my day looking down, as I think many of us do. For me, that means I look down at my phone, a computer screen, or I have my nose buried in a book. When walking down a street, I too often find my gaze directed toward the sidewalk as I scurry about. Sometimes I smile at a dog walking by my feet or peek at flowers planted nearby, and sometimes I don't. (3) I even catch myself in this mode while on a beautiful hike in the mountains. I've caught myself fixating on the ground as my feet navigate rocks and roots through the forest. It's surprisingly easy to fall into the routine of fixating my gaze on the ground. Making sure that my feet navigate the roots and rocks so that I don't trip. If I'm not aware, I can go the entire day without really looking up. But when I do, I'm always impressed by what I see.

For each of us, the sky offers a constant and ever-changing gift. During the day, the clouds shift into various shapes and shades. Some bright and buoyant and others dark and looming. A variety of trees sprinkles the woodlands with diversity which provides us with mystery and depth. From a ridgeline or the crest of a summit we can see distant horizons connected in our gaze by the ever-ending flow of mountain layers. On a clear day, with the sun burning bright, colors are enhanced in reflective shades that bend and change as it rises and sets. Never the same and always unique to the conditions of the moment. At night, the moon takes over the sky — sometimes it's barely visible, a tiny stroke of light, other times it shows up full, bright, and round. The stars glow like little lights left on to help us find our way home.

Like Thoreau, I like to walk in nature. Most times, it simply brings me joy. But when I am really caught up — in a thought, emotion, or situation — I like to remind myself to pause, listen, look around, and look up. Whatever urgency is occurring in my little brain tends to lessen. The light bending through the trees brings with it a mosaic of interests that combine to paint the perfect picture. The breeze rustling the leaves presents a soothing cadence. The sky, as it's chosen to appear, provides a backdrop that pulls it all together. Always a reminder that there's more to this world than me and my own little problems.

Thoreau's writings do the same. Old Henry David offers some sage advice. If you're so inclined, perhaps you can find some inspiration while reading his work that helps you lift your head when you feel it hanging down. Pause, listen, look around, and look up. We live in a beautiful place.

The Dawning at Lake Umbagog

In the pre-dawn hour, the world is still
Save for a few creatures, there is a quiet hush
As the first rays of sun tickle the night sky
Songbirds rustle in their nests

It starts with a subtle peep
A solitary bird sounds the prelude
In rhythmic fashion others join
An avian concerto creates a dawn chorus

Unique to the day
Harmonic tones echo in the woods
A peek out of my tent invites me in
The calm lake glows a peaceful aura

Drawn by a kaleidoscope of colors
I step into a world of solitude
Perched on a rock at the end of a point
The daily ritual unfolds before my eyes

Light flows from beyond the distant mountain
It touches the day
In the hands of an artisan
A vivid display of beauty is formed

Mist from the shoreline dances across the water
Twisting toward the sun, shapes appear

Morphing and pulsating in the gentle breeze
I delight in this recital of life

With a flick of its tail a fish crests the water's surface
The Mayfly hatch brings opportunity
Ripples emanate from the spot
In perfect cadence with the evolving day, they flow

An eagle flies toward the dawn
Gracefully making its way to a favorite fishing spot
In the calm of the moment
I hear the swoosh of his wings and sense the beat of its heart

In a state of the presence scenes unfold as they are
Some are meant to be felt
When we absorb those feelings
We then have a chance to express their impact in words

I don't pretend to know what is good for anyone else
Though I am grateful to know what is good for me
Every now and again, we get a glimpse of what's possible
The universe presents us gifts everyday

All is creation
Inside of all is change
A state of flux in perpetual motion
Within the churn comes transformation

As we navigate the daily chaos
It can be difficult to find peace
Yet a prayer unfolds in every sunrise
Being witness to that daily gift opens a gateway

With just a whisker of faith an ember sparks inside
Hope for another day can be carried within
The noise of the world melts away
In its place a deep appreciation for life fills the void

Equanimity grows when tranquil seeds are sown
In turn we get to reap a balanced existence where shadow and light coexist
The volume from the noisy world is reduced
And the voice of a perennial philosophy whispers direction

A Springtime Walk

In the quiet of the woods
Song birds sing
Chipmunks scurry about
A woodpecker drums on a dead oak tree

Trout lilies bloom
A yellow carpet spreads on the forest floor
Trilliums mix in a variety of shades
Dutchman's breeches dance in the breeze

Springtime in Vermont
An earthy fragrance in the air
Trees bud and leaves sprout
A seasonal transition works its magic

Around a corner
Where the path curves behind the cedars
A deer walks the quiet trail
It floats along

In a meditative state
I mirror its cadence
Enamored by the day
Embracing the moments

A chance meeting occurs
It brings with it a pause

Two worlds collide
We take it in

With a twitch of its tail
It sniffs the air
I return a smile
And offer a friendly nod

We lock in a gaze
One that is steeped in primal ways
Assessing each other's presence
I suppose an ancient dance of intentions

The deer makes the move
With a bow of its head
It walks off the trail
Seemingly not concerned

With a parting glance
It steps into the thicket
Camouflaged to meld into the surroundings
The majestic beast disappears

I offer a word of thanks
Though sincere
My voice seems unnatural
From the thicket a crack of a twig returns

Accepting the acknowledgment
I saunter away
Left with an appreciation of the encounter
A serene moment to ponder

Cresting the top of the hill
I walk upon the barred owl
Perched on a limb a mere 10 feet away
Its eyes reach in and touch my soul

I do my best to mimic its approach
In return the wise old bird swivels his head away
A gesture of trust
Or an act of disdain

With a quiet chuckle
I acknowledge that I'm intruding on his domain
Whispering a measure of gratitude
The beautiful bird returns a stare

I attempt to seize the moment
Trying to reflect the same calming presence
The poetic mood of the forest dictates the message
Perhaps for today a gap has been bridged

Nature brings with it a measure of integrity
Ego has no place here
Instead, a perennial philosophy sets the pace
Within it, Grace works its everlasting way

A Poem for Sherry

The beauty within each day often escapes us as we scurry along trying to catch up with society

The chase can empty us of light and leave a person feeling unfulfilled

That's why it's so important to step away every once in awhile

To soak up the essence of the new day and embrace the beauty that resonates within the rising sun

The soft light casts a warmth that touches the soul and fills the heart with grace

Then, that grace emanates from within and beams equanimous rays of kindness

It can be seen in your eyes as they are the doorway to your heart and the place where your love for life resides

It is the vessel that carries your inner beauty

That beauty then is reflected to others in the caring ways that shine through your actions

Those actions are an opening for all of us to get a glimpse of your passion for life and the true essence of your spirit

One that radiates with sweet compassion that continues to grow with each passing year

You are a beautiful soul

Your heart is as big as all outdoors and there is grace in the essence of your being

Thank you for being the wonderful person that you are!

As the Sun Sinks Low

The human condition plays within each soul
hardwired experiences tell us stories
we follow the ones that feel safe
always looking for the happy ending

Yearning for the most
subconscious pathways open possibilities
our choices set direction
a trajectory of thought projects

According to the manner of the receiver
perceptions are formed
we see them not as they are
but as we are

What we want is perfection
validation at the core
confirmation that our assumptions are real
satisfaction of the self

Rumination ensues
resentful thoughts form a defense
dualism fuels unrest
egocentric tension mounts

The pall of the moment casts a shadow
bringing the slow creep of angst

shifting the balance of consciousness
chewing the cud, we feed the sadness

We trod a well-worn trail
beaten down by normalcy
society wages war on itself
tribal law ensues

Friends part ways
families divide
personal policy creates rigid rules
pick a side and abide

We all have filters
how are they set
open to new ideas
or adjusted to conform
It takes courage to look within
deep integrity to acknowledge imperfections
gut wrenching honesty to accept what you see
awareness of a higher purpose to make a change

Too often we lack a keen sense of the obvious
the moments of the day
an appreciation for the love in our lives
acceptance and gratitude

In the gaze of a shagbark hickory
on a bluff overlooking the lake
a daily mystery unfolds
One that is beautiful and serene

As the sun sinks low into the horizon
it spreads its beneficent rays
light seeps into the shadows
it warms the cockles of the heart

Embrace the joy in life
clean the lenses
each day brings a new opportunity
sharpen your vision

Fascination is incommensurable in us
it brings a sense of interconnection
foster the blessing of awakened thoughts
stoke the hearth of your soul

A Fresh Blanket of Snow

I walk this way frequently. Yet, a fresh blanket of snow softens the woods and creates a new perspective. It comes with a pristine aura. Sounds are muffled and sunlight dances artfully through the trees. Filling open spaces with warmth and light while casting a mosaic of shadows upon a canvas of white. Trees and rocks add to the mystery of the day. They sprinkle the moments with character and bring a unique blend of colors. Mixed with the twinkle of ice coated branches within the backdrop of a cobalt blue sky, one is left with a sense of deep reverence. What a gift it is to experience a day like this. It puts a jump in my step and leaves me with a feeling of gratitude. We live in a beautiful place.

Diamond Wisdom

Sometimes when I walk around in the woods
The fog lifts and a gentle joy settles in
My human condition melts away

Moments reveal themselves
Details of my surroundings become apparent
Only then am I greeted with Divine Truth

A Perennial Philosophy echoes simplicity
Messages of profundity casts their light
The mysterious roar of silence reverberates within

A glimpse of Diamond Wisdom appears
Eloquently held in a universal heart
It cuts like a thunderbolt

Live each day well
It is the one day that we have
Tomorrow is not promised to anyone

A Morning Break

Nighttime brings a darkness
It slows the pace of life
Heads lay upon a pillow
Minds race with earthly strife

We wake up in the morning
Our feet upon the floor
The chase each day a journey
With gain a strong allure

Run your soul through the grind
Majestic views sit still
Then one morn we're struck by grace
We stop to see the thrill

The river flows from the mountain tops
Sun's rays cast a glory
This moment that I pass each day
Imbedded in my story

Many things come my way
Slow down embrace the gleaning
Love settles when we take a break
Within it find your meaning

TERRY LOVELETTE

Wisdom of the Owl

Old Wise One of the forest and sage of the ancient ways
What knowledge can you offer as I stand within your gaze

Your presence sends an aura of deep sagacity
Will mankind ever grasp a sense of your veracity

Or are we doomed to failure within our ego state
I ask of you Old Great One shed light upon our fate

We've lost a shared concern among our human race
No sapience in practice confusion in its place

Tumultuous exchanges opinions fly in vain
Divided as a nation troubled and in pain

The unrest of our times afflicts each walking soul
Angry rants abundant the impact takes a toll

From you I hear the message that falls upon my ears
The knowledge of your insight comes through loud and clear

On how we mend our problems your voice sends out a who
The healing for the misery begins with each of you

Be kind to one another with compassion at your gate
When hearts contain benevolence there is no room for hate

In Praise of Eagle Mountain

It was a beautiful morning for a walk as the sunlight danced through the trees. A stiff northerly breeze blew off the lake and chilled my face with its arctic bite.

There was a dusting of snow on the ground, and it gave the woods a warm appeal. The rock formations played well with it all while the soothing sounds from the lake below resonated within.

I find a source of comfort here at Eagle Mountain. There is a uniqueness to the solitude that's refreshingly calming. The visuals are pleasing to my eye and the silence is a welcomed friend.

Every now and again I sit and ponder life from a secluded place. I'm never disappointed with that practice.

Seems like this little corner of the world has a lot to offer this old boy. I guess I'll visit again real soon.

A Reflection on Time at Eagle Mountain

I walk this way frequently

Mostly in an attempt to find a simple joy

One that flows openly and is available to anyone at anytime

Sometimes my walk is cluttered though

Busy thoughts scoot around and stir up subconscious dust

Like the fury little dust balls found behind the sofa in spring time

They don't harm anything, they're just there

Society brings on a constant churn as it grinds away

A high-pitched whining comes along with it causing a
ringing in the ears

It settles in the air and drifts within the wind

It's only loud if I listen to it

On a good day silence and solitude are welcomed friends

They bring an inner peace

The nooks and crannies of my mind are free of little dust
balls of thought

My perception of the worldly din is abated

Instead, a relative calm governs the moments

My walk then, becomes contemplative

I'm able to consider the reality of my presence

One that is cradled in a great deal of insignificance

Yet within that truth significance exists

As I walked today, I enjoyed the fresh snow fall and a bluebird day

But I also moved about with reverence for the turf under my feet

The underlying bedrock in this location is entirely Dunham Dolomite

Irrelevant to many or maybe just simply not known

But the area lies along the Champlain Thrust Fault

It consists mostly of rock rich in calcium and magnesium carbonate

The surrounding soils a mixture of this dry rock and glacial till

Geological forces have been at play here for 500 million years or so

Phenomenal events unfolding on a time scale foreign to most of us

Seas have come and gone

In the process, the rock was morphed into various earth tones

All the while shaped into formations by the relentless flow of the shallow surf

Glacial forces furthered the effort to create the land that exists today

Dropping erratic's that have found a way to meld into the forest

While applying pressures that carved the landscape

A process of formation and reformation unfolded through the eons in a natural way

Altered further by the hands of humanity as folks toiled to form a life within a hardscrabble existence

Like the cadence of my walk and in a rhythm of its own

Nature crafted this place with a steady hand

Intricate in the detail and covered by the mask of time

It's not hard to imagine the various forms of life that have drifted through this space

Pertinent in their moments and with a significance to their insignificance

It tickles me to let these thoughts float around in my brain

They bring a healthy perspective that serves to adjust one's train of thought

Held within the divine hands of solitude a cleansing takes place

Eastern philosophies call these moments meditative

In the West, we call them moments of Grace

Call them what you will

I choose to call these moments a welcomed friend

And, a necessary part of my well-being

Whispers from the Woods

I like to roam in the wild
Not so much to escape society
Just to feel alive
To realize that I am not in control
I am but a simple man
I do my best to find appreciation each day
Sometimes I cherish the feel of the wind on my face
Warm and out of the south or a biting chill from the north
It matters little
My senses get refreshed and it clears my mind
Every ray of sunlight bending through the trees is unique
I find it fascinating to think about the journey that beam of light has made
We ignore that miracle too often
Lots of critters scampered across the snow recently
The network of trails tells a story
Today, an owl swooped over my head and landed in a nearby tree
He paused for a minute to let me enjoy his company
I heard some coyotes yelping too
In the forest, their presence echoes
I find a great deal of contentment in natural places
Apart from my tracks, I do my best to leave nothing behind
Nature does ok without me
I, on the other hand
Am lost without it.

The Dawn Chorus

I woke up early this morning to the sounds of the dawn chorus
Rubbing the sleep from my eyes and shaking the dust off my brain
My senses awakened to the day
As I listened the cacophony of song began to mix
Squawking calls blended with soft chirps
My ears opened to the melody
Waves of music wafted in the morning air
A divine harmony formed its daily symphony
My heart was touched by an avian concerto
Morning dew dripped from a fallen leaf
Spring flowers shook off the night chill
My eyes cleared through the mist
The sun peeked between the trees
Its beams cast upon my face
My skin warmed from the rays
The light activated the earth
Aromas roused from sleep filled the air
My nose picked up the smells of surrounding life
Awareness of the beauty unfolding made its way
The abundance of the moment not lost
My soul touched by an equanimous presence
A peaceful rise to the day
Coffee and warm conversation to follow
Grateful for this daily gift and blessed to be loved

Thoughts in the Snow

Snowflakes fall from the sky this morning
Autumn leaves are gone

Hillsides once dressed in vibrant colors
Now draped in a blanket of white

Singing birds muted
Wild geese absent from the sky

The woods are hushed
A wave of silence echoes in my ears

Winter brings reflective thoughts
Grateful images dance in my mind

Solitude in God's creation
Equanimous moments

Prayerful seeds sow
Grace brings its tranquil way

Footprints Left Upon the Snow

The waning sun casts a glow
Shedding light upon the snow
The path ahead framed in white
Footprints left bathed in light

Behind a track on icy trails
For each journey there is a tale
Visions form of but a few
The mind's eye creates a static view

What were the thoughts carried inside
From each traveler passing by
Good deeds and words to soothe the soul
Perhaps regrets have taken a toll

Uniquely woven within oneself
Experiences stacked on memories shelf
A common thread that humans share
An axe to grind or cross to bear

As well we have a chance to see
The good in life's eternity
Trudge the path look ahead
Embrace the journey with faith your bread

Mystery lurks within each day
Thy will, direction to lead the way
We leave our mark as we go
Like footprints left upon the snow

Walk Slowly with a Child

On a walk with our grandchildren
The world slowed
Racing thoughts focused
Discoveries of the moment appeared

Details of the day became apparent
Frozen dew drops on a leaf
Pine cones hidden in the lichen
Finding the trail an exciting mission

Everything is fresh in the mind of a child
They are here
They are now
Why aren't we?

I marvel at their curiosity
Held by gentle elegance
A spirit of exploration radiates
All is love

Lessons from these little souls
Echo through the forest
Wonder beauty awe
A natural rhythm of warmth

No one knows the future
Though many claim they do
Society sends a senseless drone
Divisive discourse a silly drivel

Leave the impulsive allure alone
In the woods you will find your place
Walk slowly with a child
Then listen for God's Grace

The Tarn

stillness of the morning the tarn is calm
reflective images from the light of dawn
somewhere a struggle of selfish thought
here at the tarn a struggle not

serene the moment as I stand in awe
the world afar so full of flaw
deep in my soul an ember sparks
ephemeral peace the ridge line stark

a fleeting joy or a lasting place
memories made a loves embrace
greater thoughts flood my brain
a simple human I resist and refrain

small speck of dust in the cosmic flow
challenging the grasp of the universal glow
what will it be as I leave from here
a joyous heart or a mind of fear

the clever muse within me plays
my gracious deity have your way
soak up the essence of the grateful morn
with warmth inside a faith reborn

accept the path as it comes my way
thy will not mine the mystery each day
my trek goes on my journey too
the tarn it seems provides a clue

Solitude in the Notch

Quite often, while walking in solitude, I'm struck with profound reverence for my surroundings. Certainly, beauty is in abundance, but the profundity goes beyond what lies on the surface. In these quiet times, the essence of existence becomes more evident. I suppose there is truth in the assertion that silence is the greatest form of prayer. Thomas Merton had some great insight to offer on this subject. Good stuff and I like to try to get out of the way while letting it all bounce around inside.

Perhaps in these moments the elements of the day conspire in some way to help wake me up just a little bit more. Whatever the case may be, I welcome the Grace and do my level best to allow it to work its way. It seems to like it more when I let things go and simply focus on my breathing.

When I do, a sense of ease finds a way to permeate through my human condition and settles into a functioning form of serenity. The resultant effect is awareness of the moments making their way. On a good day, this awareness brings with it a deep appreciation for life and my place in it. The temptation here is to explain the divine in more detail. But then I'm just another guy flapping his gums while trying to comprehend the incomprehensible. Thus, I just have faith and I do my best to lean into it. Then, I try to muster up the courage to be honest, open minded, and willing enough, to look inside myself for a deeper truth. Much of the time, reaching faith-based acceptance is the answer to all of my earthly challenges. It's also a solid litmus test that tells me the truth about where I'm at. Accepting that truth helps me understand that pointing the finger of blame elsewhere isn't an option. It's an inside job that needs to be worked out with God. A practice that I continue to be perfectly imperfect at. But I'm making some progress…

As written by Jake Owensby (a great book – *Looking for God in Messy Places*) says; "Being a person of faith is about more than clinging to this, that, or the other set of ideas. Faith is about committing ourselves to the lifelong struggle to accept the Truth. In the end, this is a struggle for freedom. Because it is only truth that will set us free." (4)

Today, as I walked along on the mountain, I felt fully alive and appreciative of my faith, my family, and my friends. It was a good day and one that I'm grateful for. A truth that I can accept.

Quiet Places

When I go to these quiet places the life of the spirit works its way within the silence of solitude, I don't question it, instead I just try to let it be. You can't cheat the spirit or the mountains. Both are brutally honest, and you have to work with the conditions to make your way.

It's not always easy, but when it comes to climbing a mountain, or with the realm of the spirit, it requires that you work, and you get uncomfortable with yourself. Progress comes from a slow, steady, and consistent effort applied by oneself. In my case I'm not graceful with either endeavor.

But somehow, I can still make my way up a mountain, and most times when I do, a gentle meditative quality seems to find me. With it comes Grace in the form of a functioning serenity, a calm mind, a loving heart, and a peaceful soul. In the beauty of that Grace comes a redeeming quality of inner strength along with the fortitude to continue to trudge the road ahead. It's true that faith without work is dead. So, I keep it simple and accept this faith-based approach to life as I continue to work my way.

Many folks that I know are struggling to find their pace in this conflicted world. Perhaps all of us can relate to being in a place of turmoil and struggle. I know that I can.

Miller Williams was a writer and poet who cut through the B.S., his writing resonates with me and gets down to the "nuts and bolts" in life. His poem compassion is a good one to consider and inspires me to look below the waves. Despite the stormy surf that we might see on the surface in one's life, each person holds within them a place of peace, their own version of divinity if you will.

In my definition, divinity is a source of light for each of us. It enables us to be the best version of ourselves that we can be. It also enables us to be present with a calm mind, a loving heart, and a peaceful soul. We simply need to be aware of this existence and be open to the hope and inspiration that rests within the moments when our inner light shines. Compassion is a gateway to accessing our divinity.

Compassion (Miller Williams)

Have compassion for everyone you meet, even if they don't want it. What seems conceit, bad manners, or cynicism is always a sign of things no ears have heard, no eyes have seen. You do not know what wars are going on down there where the spirit meets the bone. (5)

May we all find a path forward that enables each of us to be a channel of peace for others and may we do so with compassion. All the best!

Scenes Unfold

On a casual walk in the woods
Shallow light casts a glow on fresh snow
Winters sun low
Just off the horizon

It gracefully touches the forest
Bent rays of hope scattered
A tangle of silence ensues
It brings a warm presence

Dressed in the cloak of the season
Trees are sprinkled in white
Held softly in the branches
For a time cradled in care

With a wisp of wind
Flakes mist in the air
Gently falling they rest
Nestled in a crag on the rocky ledge

Patiently lying-in wait
Safe from the northerly breeze
A mounting collection forms
Blanketing the forest

As I journey
Beams of light bounce

A twinkle of diamonds dance on the snow
Scattering a natural prism of awe

Scenes unfold as they are
First glimpsed by the eye
Then gazed upon by the soul
They are seen twice

Witnessed by an audience of one
This dazzling display of nature unfolds
Marveling at the beauty in gratitude
I wonder how often this majesty goes unnoticed

Silence

In a deep chill
the woods are silent
No distractions to be heard
There is something in the silence though

Momentarily all words are shelved
The Ego struggles to be released
It finds so much comfort in words
It's only way to grasp control

Today though words were calmed
Then silence for a long moment
Just silence
It settles inside

Yet silence is not absent
Silence is not nothing
Silence is Presence
Therein lies the key

As it comes it moves away
Too many words
Too much thinking
Too much control

The chatter drowns the peace
Covering up the Presence
It dampens awareness
And then we can no longer hear

Photo by Chris Luczynski

Halo of the Setting Sun

In typical fashion, each day within the realm of social media, there is a fair amount of fightin' and bitin' going on. To each their own. Maybe someday we humans will mature enough to enable a perspective that is less divisive. Until then, we all just soldier on. I can't speak for anyone else. But I can offer a reflection from my personal experience. My path has not been straightforward nor exponential. It's been a series of starts and stops coupled with learning, unlearning, and relearning a deeper truth. So, nothing is perfected here! However, I truly believe that somewhere inside of each of us there is a place of Grace where Divine Truth exists, and the ultimate story of inner beauty is held. Here's a personal reflection for those who care to read. Thank you for the opportunity to share some of my thoughts.

Halo of the Setting Sun

In the ultimate story of beauty
Each life is graced with gifts
The grip of fear is banished
Equanimity grows

The opening of inspiration
Once shackled in repose
Springs to life in gracious moments
Embracing the universe of light

This day is a nameless friend
Born like any other
It rises to meet us
We know not what it brings

From the depth of darkness
Light shines over the horizon
Rays of hope cast shadows
They come with no demands

Spreading upon the land
Pathways of thought appear
Held gently in the bosom of creation
They wait

In time the seed of certainty will be touched
Nestled in its place
Tenderly cared for by grace
In a home of abiding love

Let the day be your calling
Turn your face toward the glow
Offer leeway to your source of intention
Inner strength will follow

In every breath lives a quiet pause
With each step a purposeful cadence
Moments of the day bring opportunity
All dwelling in silence

Yet the voice of despair echoes in every ear
It celebrates in doubt
Make friends with this misery
What glorious color it brings to your saga

As you embrace your inner truth
Acceptance spreads tendrils of courage
The halo of the setting sun brings focus
It shines bright on the magnum opus of your soul

Cocoon of Thought

O ften, I find myself caught up in a little cocoon of thought. All wrapped up in a state of self-absorbed rumination about — whatever. That's why I walk in the woods. Moving muscles changes my thoughts. The break helps me practice the pause and lets a presence much bigger than me root out the disease of society. There is seemingly a lot of that disease as it is ever present. In me and in everyone else.

It's said that each of us little human bugs process somewhere between 50,000 to 75,000 thoughts in a single day. The vast majority of these impulses are fleeting and full of noise. Yet, inside of the chaos there are opportunities for direction and additional trains of thought. Depending on our choices, new pathways of thought get presented to each of us. Within those pathways there is an endless supply of negative thoughts based in fear/hate/self-loathing as well as an endless supply of positive thoughts based in inspiration/empathy/love. Each one of us gets to choose which path we take, and the more we give from our chosen supply, is the more we get in return. While I am not a Zen Master, I believe that the essence of Karma speaks to this universal truth.

Somewhere along the line, many have forgotten that we are all in this together. Regardless of religious, political, or any other belief system; when push comes to shove - we are all in this together.

However, fear spreads its tendrils throughout each of the nearly 8 billion souls scampering about on the surface of our little planet. It casts a wide web and feeds the desires of me, me, me, and more, more, more. That fear also justifies hate. Hate of other countries, hate of different political ideologies, racial hate, religious hate, you name it -- it's all the same...Hate is Hate! Walking down the pathway of hate is a slippery slope that leads to a downward spiral - one little compromising step at a time.

Believe it or not, there is an alternative way to handle all of this madness, but we have to stop biting the hook (see Pema Chodron for more insight). We have become conditioned to respond in certain ways. Repeatedly taking action against each other widens the divide. As emotional and self-serving as those actions are, most of the time, they do little but add to the drama bubbling at the surface in our society today. I'm not suggesting that we divorce ourselves of opinion but suggesting that we temper our assumptions and perhaps we could stop painting with a broad brush. We are all quick to jump to the same conclusions, over and over again, where we justify our feelings by siding with those that think like us.

It is hard to look in the mirror and do an honest self-appraisal, and for some, it might not be possible. Changing our conditioned responses is a difficult process to engage in. It comes with traps and pitfalls. Certainly, it's much easier to point the finger and lay the blame elsewhere. But how effective is that action? Is it always the other thing or another person? Or do each one of us have some skin in the game here too?

Extending a hand in loving kindness makes us vulnerable. Indeed, it comes with risk and the thought of taking that action can send shivers up your spine. However, you might find that acting from a place of love (instead of hate) is just what the doctor ordered.

As author Susan Piver wrote: Generosity is a gesture of power. Instead of biting the hook of aggression or numbness, there is another way. Try helping someone else or listening with an understanding ear. There are plenty of people in the world in need of help and a little empathy. We don't have to look hard or search in far-away places. Reaching out to help another human being is a positive action that benefits them, but it is good for you too. We don't have to sit with our fears, and we are not powerless. Be generous with kindness and love. We all win when we do that. It's the premise behind the golden rule. (6)

Further, our lives, home, family, friends, workplace, body, our unique abilities are all part of our kingdom. We have command of that kingdom, and we get to make choices. Fears, anxiety, and self-centered desires aside, what loving actions can we take to ensure that we have our own world in order? I don't know about you, but I have plenty of work to do, my kingdom is not perfect.

As mentioned above, we are all in this together. There is no place in America (or in the world) for the madness that's being played out. Having said that, human nature will have us pointing fingers at this juncture. What we should be doing is asking ourselves some tough questions instead. How am I responding? Am I feeding the madness with my own hate or am I working toward a better world through loving kindness? As tough as it is to recognize, our actions matter, and perfection of self is a lofty goal attained by no one. If there is confusion about what action to take, then consider that our thoughts become our actions. Thinking better thoughts will lead to better actions, better actions will result in a better world for ourselves and others. Putting our best foot forward each day isn't easy. But we can choose to work on progress instead of perfection.

Ultimately, it is what it is for each of us. Channeling Maya Angelou: we know what we know, and we don't know what we don't know, however, once we know better, we should be better. (7) But let's not pretend. Sometimes we are scared, sad, angry, or shocked. Sometimes, life is overwhelming, and we hit the apex of our ability to cope. As humans, we all have it within us to reach that point. If we can just consider raising our awareness of the results of our actions, it might enable us to not bite the hook when we are about to blow our top. It might prevent us from lashing out with aggression and intolerance. It's possible that we can choose love over hate more often. How, or if, each of us does this remains a personal choice. Some choose prayer, some meditation, or maybe it just comes down to looking at ourselves in the mirror each day to maintain an awareness that our actions do matter, and that today, I'm choosing to not feed the madness. If one decides to take that action repeatedly, over and over again, new pathways of thought will open up and productive actions will occur. Books like the Bible shed additional light on this topic.

We the people can do remarkable things when we stick together. That quality is what makes us great. No politician or ideology can give us that because we already have it. In my humble opinion it is beyond the time to realize this truth and act accordingly.

Peace and prosperity to all and may God Bless us with his love.

Deeper Thoughts from A Walk

Mount Mansfield is a beautiful centerpiece here in Vermont. Grand and glorious anytime of the year. But winter seems to pull the beauty out from within the mountain. Looking from the west, its snow-covered summit looms above the Champlain Valley. Its face outlined magnificently as its gaze is fixed on the heavens. It greets those who visit with a wind whipped landscape and a biting cold that warns you to not linger. Yet graciously, it gives a blessing to anyone willing to listen. When you do, you learn more about yourself and leave with a piece of the mountain tucked away safely in your soul. I am grateful for mountain days and appreciate the blessings that the hills so freely hand out.

On this day though I walked with a mood of melancholy. Although I enjoyed my walk and the beautiful place that I get to live in, my thoughts, prayers, and sympathies are with the people of Ukraine. Especially the children. Their struggles with violence and aggression are more difficult than the climb up any mountain. While the chances are slim, I have hope that evil hearts eventually find a pathway to peace. Although that epiphany may not come until many souls are lost and perhaps only 5 seconds before their last breath. Hope remains that the human condition will mature past the point of self-destruction. May even the most callous heart find the resolve to look in the mirror, experience a moment of clarity, and become open to allowing faith in their True Self to drive away their fear.

Believe as you will. I am not pushing an ideology. Instead, I hope to offer a reminder that each one of us, me included, can and should be better. To repeatedly engage and promote a divisive discord is to fuel the flames of evil that burn within the darkness inside of each one of us. Conversely, our True Self allows our inner light to shine. Deep within human nature is where the source of that light exists. For you, me, and for every other human being currently walking on our planet. Even those that feed the madness. If I feed the madness that means me, and if you feed it, that means you. Having the courage to look deep enough to find your own truth is the beginning of a better world for each person as well as the rest of humanity. Within that journey you find the switch that allows your inner light to shine on the darkest part of your own soul. May each one of us be brave enough to take that journey. Otherwise, the cycle of evil will continue to work its way within you as it has throughout our human existence.

As John Steinbeck wrote in 1941 as WWII was raging: "Not that I have lost any hope. All the goodness and the heroisms will rise up again, then be cut down again and rise up. It isn't that the evil thing wins — it never will — but that it doesn't die. I don't know why we should expect it to. It seems fairly obvious that two sides of a mirror are required before one has a mirror, that two forces are necessary in man before he is man" (8)

Like our rugged little mountain, I vow to stand strong. To repeatedly look in my mirror, make sure that my own house is in order, then weather the storms, and continually keep my gaze on the heavens. I love the State of Vermont and I love the United States of America. But my devotion doesn't stop there. Similar perhaps to Diogenes; my affiliation goes beyond the dualistic lines impulsively drawn by society "I am a citizen of the world". As a result of this truth, I'm at a place where I need to pick a side. Thus, I will not side with evil. In fact, I will not rationalize it or show evil any praise. Instead, I will continue to do my best to keep space in my heart for empathy and kindness. Then make sure that I walk that talk. After all, Jesus, Buddha, the Shamans, the Mystics, the Mountains, and the Children, expect nothing less.

The Path of the Heart

A steady rain pelts
The forest welcomes it in
Soothing rhythms
Solemn mist

The fresh canopy of spring
Striving for life
A pitter-patter cadence
Whispering in the solitude

A million seedlings dance in delight
Each drop of water a celebration
Opportunity to grow
A chance to be

Earthworms forage in the slippery soil
Munching on microbes
Absorbed in their purpose
Fattening up after the torpid days of winter

A robin plucks away at the forest floor
Nestlings hatched
Responsibilities to fulfill
Bountifully harvesting from the banquet of life

Contemplative thoughts flow
Prayer resonates within
Meditative moments
Life in abundance

Restorative inspiration
Grace filled experiences
Freely available
The way of the peaceful warrior

Walk the path of the heart
Let it be now
It is your time to renew
The great mystery awaits

Contemplative Thoughts

As always, I leave my walks better for the experience. For me, nature just works that way. Gradually, throughout my walk, I contemplate one of the morning meditations that I read. I find that the thoughts incubate into meaning when they process in a natural rhythm. Not for everyone I suppose but a practice that works for me. Sometimes clear direction finds a way to bubble to the surface of my reality during my walk. While other times, it takes a little bit longer. It's not up to me to determine the spiritual timeline. It's up to me to have faith. Then to realize that my attitude toward the life I'm living can have a tangible, measurable, and profound effect on how I respond to the events of the day. That's why it's important for me to accept that I only get a daily reprieve that is contingent on the maintenance of my spiritual condition. Spending quiet time with God each day opens up a pathway to insight and direction that exists beyond my ego self. If that's the only revelation that came from my walk today, then I'll rest with it and be grateful. We live in a beautiful place...

The Courage to Change

In silence the world exists. Perhaps, even, this is the moment for which you were created. To stop for that moment. To put down the distractions. To resist the urge to, yet again, get muddled up in expectations, opinions, and societal norms. Systems tell us who we should be. What successes we should focus on. How we should be living. What we should love, and conversely, what to hate. If we can pause long enough, a miracle happens. Grace ushers in an awareness. It allows us the freedom to look at it and realize that it isn't about me. That I am just a small, interconnected part of a much bigger whole. The questions then become; do I have the courage to listen? If I do, will I have the courage to change?

Seasons of Change

Seasons change in Vermont
Persistent natural rhythms
Variations present experiences
A range of shifting states
Flora and fauna flourish
Majestic in their ways

In summer's heat
We long for cooler days
Beads of sweat
Humid air
Stickiness wicks the day
Its presence bemoaned

Long days of warmth
Nature in abundance
Soon air waxes crisp
Dew drops lay heavy on the grass
Daylight wanes
Longer nights ensue
A natural occurrence in earths orbital dance with the sun

Vibrant colors sprinkle the hillsides
A celebration of sorts
With it the landscape softens
Artistic presentation from a higher order
Magnificence
Spellbinding beauty

Short and sweet is autumns glow
A captivating radiant mosaic
We stand in awe
For but a moment
Transformative winds blow change
Trees ready for the cold

Breezes shift slowly to the north
Raindrops pelt a vigorous cadence
The mountain ambiance warns of winter
Nightfall temps flip the switch
First snow falls
A blanket of white cradles the land

Time slows as winter settles in
Throw another log on the fire
Warm a cup of cocoa
Embrace the quiet in the fresh falling snow
Ponder the beauty held within each snowflake
Nurture reflective thoughts in reverence

As the sun arcs higher in the sky
A gradual shifting occurs
Air warms
Snowpacks release their life-giving resource
Seeds tucked away in repose awaken
Life stirs in the secret underworld of nature
A crack is formed through the warmed crust of earth
With the strength of a cosmic flow

A sprout reaches upward
Compelled to live
Pulled by a universal force
Flowers sprinkle color on the forest floor

The perpetual cycle of life continues
It's timeline seldom known in the chase of a busy world
Moments of meaning offered
Gifts within each season of life
Pause often
Appreciate the everlasting Grace

What Do You See on the Forest Floor

In the very heart of nature
Where the rhythm of creation rules
Amidst the complex pull of forces
Lives a world mysterious to man

The understory of the forest
Works the cycle of life
An achievement of order
Against all odds and its blithe abandonment

Faces of the seasons
Expressively subtle
Couched in normalcy
Quietly perfecting its craft

When winds bring their change
When winter weeps another snow
And the flowers bend in sorrow
What do you see on the forest floor

A transcendent flow of necessity
Is it a possibility
That right there, in a flower
One can find the meaning of life?

The Gift of Reciprocity

Walking slowly along the trail
Head bent low
Eyes focused on the ground
Life in abundance greets me

Ephemerals sprout from their winters rest
Carolina Spring beauty, Bloodroot, Trout Lily, Dutchman's Breeches, Trillium
Various colors sprinkle the forest floor
They mix well with the Fiddlehead Ferns, Ramps, and Skunk Cabbage

A fresh fragrance drifts in the breeze
Somewhat sweet
Occasionally pungent
It smells of renewal and life

We hear it time and again
Sounds from a restless society
Where do we find meaning?
How do we seek hope?

Rushing at a frantic pace
Enthralled by the daily chase
How do we connect in this broken world?
Is it possible to find the strength to live fully?

In the disconnected oneness of the daily grind
You can get swallowed up

Lost in the churn of chaos and confusion
Blind to the beauty that waits right in front of your eyes

Do we not have an obligation to receive these gifts of beauty, awe,
and wonder?
W. B. Yeats wrote, "The world is full of magic things, patiently
waiting for our senses to grow sharper."
Strikingly poignant
Life, waiting and hoping to be noticed

Yet, we pass it by
Lost in thought
Too busy with an agenda of nothingness
In a hurry to get nowhere

Intentionally dulling the senses
It helps us endure another day
Unsettled and a little lost
A penchant for melancholy fills the void
What if we take another course
Pause and appreciate brief moments of beauty
Let the wonders and awe of nature steep
Allow the renewal of life to nourish our inner grace

Maybe these moments can offer us strength
Perhaps even bring to us a deep and abiding connection of the
world we live in
It's possible then for new pathways of thought to open up
Inspirations that are fueled by the interconnected Grace that binds
it all together
When we honor Mother Earth by accepting her gifts
We move toward that interconnected Grace
Gratitude for life and one's place in it swells up within
Reverence of the experience shines rays of hope

As we receive these gifts, we long to offer some of our own
It's possible that you might find yourself listening ever more closely
to the natural world
What does it offer? What does it need? What is it asking of us?
Compassion saunters in and the spirit of reciprocity starts to form

These interconnections make us stronger, more resilient, more
hopeful
Loneliness is abandoned and solitude embraced
In these quiet spaces
Silence brings insightful meaning

Acceptance hints the answers
With beauty comes loss
For every joy a hurtful sorrow
Waves of awe bring wonder and dark winds blow in the confusion of
grief

All part of the wounded world and our tenuous human condition
Often in the woundedness we hold on
Barely sometimes and frequently kicking and screaming
Fighting for joy amongst the despair

Options exist for each of us
There are choices to make
I acknowledge the difficulties of life
But gratefully I choose the pursuit of joy

Not because my head is buried in the sand
But because joy is abundant in the world
It comes to me as the gift of Grace throughout the day
As best I can, within my human condition, it's incumbent on
me to return it (9)

A Walk with the Birds

The world is a busy place. In the course of a normal day, it will have us running from the start while maintaining constant contact with our electronic devices. Amazingly, that little handful of electrons, microns, and molecules has a firm grip on society. So much so that the simple joys in life, and their many gifts, take a back seat. Instead, the chase ensues, and the impulsive allure brought on by the excitement of the grind rules the moments. Within that grind is a world that settles into an argumentative place. Strong opinions abound, and human pride makes us want to be right, be heard, and get in the last word. It is said that even Jesus, Buddha, The Mystics, The Stoics, and The Shamans argued too. But that they did it gently and with the simple intention of teaching wisdom-based lessons. (10) Lessons that I repeatedly need to learn.

Ironically, some of that learning comes through my dreaded electronic devices. I routinely tap into the world of electrons, microns, and molecules. I've found that these little jewels of our modern times are portals to an endless supply of wisdom-based lessons that are steeped in a Perennial Philosophy which provide anyone who cares to listen some measure of equanimity. Of course, they are also portals to an endless supply of drama, chaos, and confusion. Thus, I get to make a choice about which path I take and what state of mind I choose to live in. I suppose that everyone gets to make that same choice.

Admittedly, it can be difficult for me to sort out the path of a peaceful attitude amidst the clamor of emotionally charged exchanges that run riot in our daily chase. Again, I get to make a choice. Do I engage in chaos or go for a walk? Most days, I choose to shut down the screen and saunter into the woods. The nudging to take that action comes from a power greater than me, and at times, it graciously allows me to walk in contemplation. While my Ego tells me the opposite, my soul ushers me out the door and into the realm of the spirit. Perhaps wisdom bestowed from the lessons of Perennial Philosophy does for me that which I can't do for myself? I tend to think so. Wallow in apathy or walk with hope? Another choice.

Hermann Hesse offers some sage advice: "…to the person suffering from lack of time and from apathy; Seek out each day as many as possible of the small joys, and thriftily save up the larger, more demanding pleasures for holidays and appropriate hours. It is the small joys first of all that are granted us for recreation, for daily relief and disburdenment, not the great ones." (11)

Yesterday, I found these small joys in the woods and from the mouths of various songbirds. All that was required of me was to be there and be present. The Scarlet Tanager, The Wood Thrush, The Wrens, The Robins, and The Red Breasted Grosbeaks did the rest. Their collective songs filled the air with a Divine Presence. Small joys and gifts freely given.

From my electronic device came the following meditation: "For the gift of this day, I give thanks. Whatever is mine to give, let me give generously, mindful of the abundant Spirit of service and love within me. Whatever is mine to receive, let me claim it gratefully, knowing I am worthy of all the good the Universe showers upon me. Whatever is mine to learn, let me receive gently the understanding of Spirit with an open mind and heart. Whatever is mine to forgive, let me allow the flow of healing Love to free me and release any pain I hold. At the end of this day, may my heart be filled, my hands emptied and my mind at rest." (12)

Yesterday was a good day and I slept with gratitude. When I awoke this morning, I was able to give thanks in appreciation. I'm fortunate that I get another crack at life today and the potential to realize the small joys and little gifts that await just around the corner. May you take the opportunity to realize the small joys and little gifts of your own. We live in a beautiful place.

Why We Wake

I don't know what today will bring
A flood of thoughts one thousand things

Slow it down give it space
Just try it once see the grace

That tree on the knoll might catch the eye
Or the beauty of the still in a clear blue sky

Sometimes the sun just bounces through
The cloud covered hills a majestic hue

Accustom yourself to the world around
Majestic views our land abounds

The scent of freshness in the morning air
Moments that ease and sooth despair

Say yes to the glory that awareness brings
The songbirds know that's why they sing

Pay it heed and ease the rush
Opened ears hear the hush

In a gradual way we see inside
That place of peace in all resides

From there we hear the quiet voice
Heartfelt directions toward a choice

Fuel the chase with another rant
Or embrace this moment, take the chance

When you do, small joys appear
Many and often it all comes clear

Bonus gifts are carried away
They continue to give throughout the day

That's why we wake and look about
It fills the soul and removes self-doubt

Divine Presence heaven sent
The cost to me one moment spent

A Mountain Reflection

The mountains don't preach
Instead for millions of years they sit in prayerful silence
Cradled in the arms of creation
Granite Buddha's sending subtle messages of hope
Come close, hear the stillness
Let it flow through your fearful soul
Open your eyes in reverence
See the beauty of the day
Accept your small and simple self
Like the mountains, you belong
Heed the divine voice of your conscience
Bow to the spirit of the creator
Walk the path with confidence
In the journey you find your purpose

Silent Conversation

One of the many joys of a contemplative walk in the mountains is the chance to be alone with your thoughts. It's not the lonely isolation that it might seem.

Yet, if one is caught up in the churn of a busy world, then the strain of loneliness tugs at the core. With that pull comes a persistent feeling of emptiness which can cause fear and separation. Then, the relentless force of isolation rules the day. In the busy world we are blinded by the Ego and our senses are dulled.

Contemplation ushers in a source of Intention that opens up a silent conversation. One that offers companionship and direction. It brings a friendship with the created world that has been with us since the dawn of time. A thoughtful solitude awakens a sense of privilege in the heart and an appreciation for the abundant life of the present moment. Each day we have a chance to see the precious gifts with the eye of the soul. If only we have the courage to get out of the way, listen to the silence, and let the blessings wake us up.

Summer Solstice

Today is the summer solstice in the northern hemisphere and the day that the sun is at its zenith. Somewhere up there behind the clouds it beams at full power. Below the clouds we still celebrate life. The beauty of light that bounces through the cosmos and refracts at the water's surface. Shadows that bend into the edges of the hillside and define the layers of geology that form the Green Mountains. In these mountains comes a manifestation of life. Colorful and abundant. Always available to show the way of Grace that presents itself freely. Even on a sunless day, there beams a gracious light. We live in a beautiful place…

A Hidden Field

Somewhere amidst the trees you'll find it
A hidden field where the grass grows thick

I can't explain how to get there
You need to seek it on your own

But when you crest the rise of hope
You'll see the amber waves

Rippling wisps of wind whisper a song
They beckon a responsive dance

Strands of different lengths sway
A natural rhythm of wonder opens

It won't appear in an anguished mind
Weed filled thoughts choke out the vision

A calloused heart will yield no beauty
It casts a pall of misery

The disillusioned soul is empty
Drained of joy it sees no glory

Yet faint rays of optimism show the way
A secret place awaits

No one there to mow it down
The flowers bloom

From afar it's hard to see
Nestled in safety

Among the weeds
They work a magic beauty

The wisdom of nature
In a display known only by the spirit

All in a purposeful way
Shining a universal light

The above poem was written after a recent walk. One where I contemplated these twisted times through which we are living. It occurred to me that beauty always exists amidst the chaos and confusion brought on by dark actions of disillusioned souls. While I don't turn a blind eye to evil acts, I can't become the proverbial monster that we all want to slay. Thus, I can't fight evil acts of another with evil acts of my own. If I do, evil wins. Instead, I'm committed to continue to make attempts at turning on the light of awareness. Each day and one day at a time. While my attempts may be trivial in the long run, they seem sane to me, and they provide me with a meaningful purpose. Imagine a world where each one of us little bugs did the same...

"How does one cope with evil? Not by fighting it but by understanding it. In understanding, it disappears. How does one cope with darkness? Not with one's fist. You don't chase darkness out of the room with a broom, you turn on a light. The more you fight darkness, the more real it becomes to you, and the more you exhaust yourself. But when you turn on the light of awareness, it melts." —Anthony De Mello (13)

In Solitude

It was an enjoyable walk this morning at one of my favorite spots. Today, Laraway was especially welcoming. I attempted to take it all in so that I might save it for future moments to reflect on. Maybe for a time when the hustle and bustle of life ushers in a chaotic pace or perhaps when the drone of society becomes an annoyance. At those times, I need to remember this beauty so that I can feel this sense of awe and make sure that I allow it to help me stay centered within myself. Sometimes, this recall is too easy to forget. A walk in the woods gives me opportunities to remember.

Surely, if I'm consumed with thoughts of other things then I'll miss the majestic works of nature that are the low hanging fruit. Little morsels of serenity eloquently placed in their natural environment existing and being what they are. Just a whisker of awareness lets it in. A little sliver of appreciation for the life and beauty that is on display each day, one day at a time, and within every moment. Letting go and letting God, that's really all that it takes.

When I do, I notice things. The reflections of the world held within the arms of a mud puddle. The constant chatter of water rushing through the mountain streams that surround me, a primal sound of reassurance that all was well. The soothing sound of the breeze rustling in the canopy. Its sway shakes loose rain drops left from yesterday's storm. They fall with a pitter-patter cadence that brings a refreshing mist to the forest as it collects into a cloud of fog. The feel of the air on my face, a combination of the cool mountain morning and the warmth of the rising sun. Invigorating and vibrant, it fueled the muscles in my old legs and brought joy to every step. It also presented breathtaking moments of beauty. Pausing for a breather, I met the lizard of Laraway. His grace and elegance on full display as we exchanged good tidings. All of this here all along as if patiently waiting to be noticed.

In solitude, I saw it all, I heard it all, I felt it all, and it was very enjoyable. Fulfilled, there I stood, grateful for this moment of existence. We live in a beautiful place!

The Mud Puddle

It looks so placid
Why would anyone want to stir it up
Let it be
Enjoy what you see

But one thousand influences beckon
Outside powers at work
The impulsive trigger at the ready
Convinced that it's our duty

Jump in the puddle
Splash around
Sling a little mud
Keep the great illusion going

It's your duty
To carry the hammer
Be at the ready
Pounce when the buzz words come

Lapse into your conditioned response
Your fight to be right
Justified in self-centered desires
It quells a sense of isolation

It feels good to vent
A cleansing occurs
When we project our angst
Scapegoat your way to freedom

The ego revels in victory
But for a brief moment in time
The slow creep of angst
Echoes unrest

Our mind becomes a battlefield
In search of peace
Groping for reconciliation
We live unresolved

In a state of confusion
Torn in two
The false self of society
And the true self of Grace

The residue of hubris
A flood of destruction created
Debris strewn about
Emotional litter scattered

Funny little creatures we are
Joys and sorrows
Likes and dislikes
Colored by the company we keep

Biased in destruction
Strong public feelings flow
There is amnesia in the allure

It clouds our true aspirations

In a befuddled state
We flounder
How do we fix the misery
It will take a miracle

Not the walking on water kind
But a shift in perspective
Making a decision to change
A revelation of our own actions

Then the real miracle has room to blossom
By dropping the stick
We start to see things with some clarity
And we stop stirring up the mud puddle

Let it go
Let it settle
Let it reflect into you
Let it know that its beauty has been felt

In that place
Everything is a miracle
Especially true
When it grows in you

It's Always There

Somewhere tucked within it stirs
Even in the blithest most lighthearted folks
A fundamental dis-ease churns
An unquenchable fire renders

Leaving the vast majority of us incapable
Or even remotely aware in this life
Of ever coming to full peace

In the marrow of our bones
Lurking in the deepest inner regions
Nestled within the soul
Lies a yearning desire

For eons the greats have echoed
Literature, poetry, art, philosophy, psychology, religion
All attempt to name and analyze
The incessant effervescent longing

Elusively it maneuvers
Ever evading its discovery
Gnawing away
Eroding the calm

Seldom is it touched
Rarely is it known
Daily it works
Always in a rush

Fed by the modern world
A Phantasmagoria of entertainments
Obsessions…
Addictions…
Distractions…
Of every sort

Like a jack-in-the-box
The tension mounts
Spring loaded emotions
Impulsive reactions occur

What to do
When it's you

The mundane existence
Of a simple soul
Finitude and mortality
Confined within walls

Turn to the awe in the splendor of things
Seek the beauty that the songbirds sing
Gaze at the dawning of a new born day
Find reverence on a mountain
It will show the way

Beside the turmoil of the longing place
Quietly waiting for the chaos to stop
Gently persuading a mindful thought
Rests the serenity of eternal Grace
It's always there
Just for you (14)

May you find it too

A Meaningful Existence

It's good to get away sometimes
To see the world from a new perspective

Fresh eyes open
The sleep gets washed away

Clouded vision clears
Purposeful direction follows

Inner transition blossoms
Regaining a sense of life

A journey of discovery awakens
Sound rhythm churns within

Traveling with reverence
Allows the richness of life to unfold

Little moments of beauty
Sprinkle the days

Light shines a warm glow
Grace presents awareness

The soul becomes energized
It feeds the heart contentment

It's also good to come home
To recognize the familiar

The contrasting journeys
A blend of graciousness

An adventure of beauty
Felt at the core

Glorious reflections
Deep colors of our life

A meaningful existence
Held gently within the solitude

Cradled in the arms of silence
Patiently waiting for you

Equanimity and Grace

I enjoy quiet but brisk hikes up Laraway mountain. With the seasons shifting, it was a good day to be alive. We live in a beautiful place...

The last vestiges of summer
Holding tight

Night air chills
The pull of autumn

Working a subtle way
Patiently persistent

It touches the forest
One leaf at a time

Green tints waver
Pigments shift

Yielding to the season
Vibrant colors emerge

In a rhythmic cadence
Transformation follows

Spiced scents of decay
The ripe fragrance of fall

Nature's cycle of life
Quiet and mellow

It prepares in silence
An impassioned response
In a great celebration
On full display

A brief appearance
In shifting form

Beauty and glory
Equanimity and Grace
Watch in wonder
Let it soothe your soul

Spencer's Ledge

I make no secret about my love for the mountains. For me they are a place of reverence. I've found that they repeatedly send messages of hope that are filled with an appreciation for life, gratitude, and interconnected truth. Grace, if you will, that's available to anyone who listens to the heartfelt silence. So, I walk while enjoying the quiet solitude.

To the best of my abilities, within my human condition, I try to simply be present in these serene settings. When I'm in that space, the universe often provides gateways of inspiration that lead to pathways of contemplative thought. Gifts freely given if I remain open and teachable. Today's inspiration came from a sign hung at the ledges on Spruce Peak.

I have a fond connection to this location. Over the years I've visited this spot often with Sherry or by myself. It's sort of like a backyard getaway that's comfortable, easy to reach, trustworthy, and dependable.

With an active sky and low hanging clouds the views on this day were less than spectacular. Still, I forged ahead and walked out on the ledge. Knowing the place quite well, I immediately noticed a wooden sign hanging on a tree. From a distance my 60 something eyes couldn't make out the words, but I recognized the prominent trout in the center of the sign. Curious and intrigued I walked over to the sign to get a closer look.

Reading the words choked me up. The words on the sign read "Spencer Morton"; "Pursuit of Unattainable Perfection". From what I learned later; those were words that Spencer used to describe fly fishing. A sport that he had built his life around in Jackson Hole Wyoming before passing away suddenly from an aortic aneurysm in May of 2021 at the age of 38. A passing that came with great sadness for anyone who knew Spence. Heartfelt condolences continue to go out to his family and close friends.

I knew Spencer from a different time and a different sport. It was my good fortune to be part of the coaching staff for the University of Vermont Men's Ice Hockey team when Spencer played there in the early 2000's. He was as genuine as they come. His friendship was real and not manufactured. In fact, he had the unique ability to bring that friendship always through an act of kindness and recognition. Because of his unique genuine nature, he left an indelible mark on me. I'm certain that he did the same thing with each person he encountered along the way.

Spruce Ledge is no longer a place that I will frequent. For evermore it will be known as Spencer's Ledge to me, and each visit will be an opportunity to remember the spirit of a remarkable human being. May your grace and interconnected truth continue to inspire us all.

A Time of Transition

In the woods leaves lay to rest in a carpet of color
Shifting seasons
A time of transition
In silence the way of nature keeps pace with the cosmic flow
Running within a cycle of creation
Living, dying, and rebirth happening in rhythm
Without the slightest care of public opinion
Whitman's test of wisdom
Felt in the depths
Unable to be passed on
A certainty of the reality and immortality of things
Held in excellence
Offered in the float of sight
Brought into the senses
Under the clear blue sky and the spacious clouds
It prospers in the landscape
Flowing currents of the divine
Provoking a response
From the deepest regions of the soul
It lingers in its place
Patiently in search of someone to pay attention

Taking Time to Go Within

In the little miseries of life
A cacophony of the world's troubles brew
It can be difficult to find quiet

Have you ever felt the urge to run
To leave it all behind

Perhaps instead go within
Find the tranquil place
Silence yourself with prayer

Take a path through the shadows
Let in the restorative sun
Welcome the beam on your face
Feel the wind
Smell the earth
Turn slowly away from this bruised world

For a moment leave it behind
The deafening sirens of suffering
The din of restlessness
The angst of ire in another bitter rant

Abandon the urge to respond
Let the calling of serenity show the way

Going out is going in
Drop the need to control
Abandon the fear
Let go of the pain

Find that airy place
Where the sunlit path leads
Blending with the shadows
To form the divine mystery of peace

There is a freedom in the calm
A restful strength
It will find its way within

Fueling your resolve
Restoring your energy
Enabling the way of equanimity

With newfound courage
Thy will be done
Take the first steps
To the uttermost
Return that peace to the world

TERRY LOVELETTE

A Morning Walk

A morning walk in Autumns glow
Pristine images capture the mind

Lungs at work, breathing steady's
Pace governed by a meditative cadence

The call of a loon echoes from the lake below
Wild and haunting, a more wondrous sound may not exist

Sunlight flickers through the trees
Artwork of a higher order ever present

Embracing the majesty of divine love
Senses are heightened

A mosaic of colors presents a magical glow
Expressions of nature's beauty abound

Reverence rests within the heart
Serenity soothes the soul

A Hidden Wholeness

O n my walk yesterday, I came upon a lady making her way off a hill. Although steep and leaf covered this woman was adroitly navigating the trail in a manner that seemed younger than her age, which I estimated to be in the late 70's/early 80's. As I approached, she was pulling out her cell phone and only looked my way when I said hello. Smiling, she said I need to text my husband to remind him to be careful while descending the hill. She was concerned that the slippery leaves might cause him to fall. I mentioned that I was heading up the hill and would be happy to share her concern with her husband. She took me up on the offer. So, I asked for a brief description of her partner in case I met more than one person on my ascent. She laughed and said, he's the really old guy with walking sticks. In a quick response I said that on any given day her description would suit me quite well. Seemingly amused, she shook her head and said, "He's much older than you." With a tip of my hat, I said fair enough, and moved on

Soon I came upon a gentleman who fit her description to a T. I recognized him immediately. We had bumped into each other on other occasions and have exchanged pleasantries about the beautiful location that we get to walk through. Interactions of this type are often brief, somewhat superficial, and tend to fade from your memory quickly. But others seem to linger with you and form a favorable imprint. Interactions of this type come with a grounding presence that ushers in a familiarity and a relative ease. Although I didn't even know his name, my interactions with this gentleman had left that favorable imprint. I felt like I was seeing an old friend.

I estimate that this gentleman is in his late 80's/early 90's and he is still able to make his way along some lower elevation wooded paths. That fact alone is impressive enough. The fact that he does it with a smile on his face bigger than the outdoors is true inspiration and captivating. As we warmly welcomed each other's presence, we introduced ourselves by name for the first time. In my view, an introduction that felt overdue but thoroughly natural. It was lovely to officially meet David.

I mentioned that we had chatted briefly on a couple of other occasions. His smile and nod were affirmation enough. I let him know that I appreciated those interactions and that I sensed his joy of the outdoors. With a great deal of sincerity in his voice and a look of integrity in his eyes he said that he has a deep reverence for nature. He went on to describe his adoration for the beauty and immensity of it all. He recalled some of his hiking adventures on the Long Trail, the Pacific Crest Trail, and other locations. Then he spoke about how impactful these experiences can be if one is open to the hidden wholeness that they bring into your life. He went on to say that one can become changed for the better if they allow that spirit to sort out the unnecessary churn in life and instead focus on a path forward with compassionate kindness. Sometimes, he said, the best I can do is to go home and try to capture the essence of it all in a poem. With a twinkle in his eyes, he said I don't know how good I am with it, but it's a process that allows me to express myself and find a deeper truth. I thanked him for his time and his insight. I also let him know that I completely identified with his experiences, wisdom, approach, and appreciation of it all. True gifts to contemplate as I continue on in the interconnected journey that we all travel.

As we were parting ways, I informed him of the message from his wife. With a deep belly laugh he said at one point in time that type of message would have bothered the hell out of him. But that today, he's grateful to recognize it as a message of compassion, kindness, and love.

What incredibly solid insight and a gift of wisdom to experience. One that is vitally important for all of us who are concerned about our society. To look at oneself and arrive at a clear and cogent statement of our ills so that we can correct them. If we don't then our efforts stay focused on superficial symptoms of things that are not even related directly to the illness of our world. In countless ways the remedies that so many of us emote about are expressions of the sickness itself.

Trappist monk Thomas Merton wrote words of wisdom in his book (Witness to Freedom: The Letters of Thomas Merton in Times of Crisis) about how the interconnectedness and deepest truths transcend all boundaries and worldly limitations.

"I would almost dare to say that the sickness is perhaps a very real and very dreadful hatred of life as such, of course subconscious, buried under our pitiful and superficial optimism about ourselves and our affluent society. But I think that the very thought processes of materialistic affluence (and here the same things are found in all the different economic systems that seek affluence for its own sake) are ultimately self-defeating. They contain so many built-in frustrations that they inevitably lead us to despair in the midst of "plenty" and "happiness" and the awful fruit of this despair is indiscriminate, irresponsible destructiveness, hatred of life, carried on in the name of life itself. In order to "survive" we instinctively destroy that on which our survival depends." (15)

Compelling truths to ponder. There is an egregious bombardment of negativity in the "normal" flow of society today and in recent years. No need to expand upon it, it's a well-documented machine of insanity. Seemingly, a playground where many folks oddly feel some type of connection and validation. So be it. As for me, a contemplative walk in the woods brings about a measure of humility and lends the cure to my human condition. It brings about the hidden wholeness that folks like Thomas Merton and my friend David allude to. I'm all in with that approach to life…

An Old Friend

A familiar landscape is like an old friend. It welcomes you in while allowing space for comfort and ease. Always, there is much to catch up on and the process of reacquainting ensues. Although the exchange of communication transcends the realm of normal human interaction it flows with insight and meaning.

In the mountains, senses become heightened, and the voice takes its place as a nonessential item. Eyes shift and focus on the beauty of the day. Accentuated by the sun's lower position in the late fall November sky, light casts shadows that bend in a reflective recital of life. Imbedded into the vibrant greens of Vermont's mountain mosses, the rays beam a graciousness throughout this serene alpine setting. A cool breeze blows steadily from the north touching the hills with an arctic caress. A reminder of winter's arrival, ice forms in the shadows, quietly complying to the inevitable flow of the seasons. Breath mists in the cold, skin absorbs the chill of gusting winds, it whistles in the ears. Successfully, it casts a warning that sends an intuitive response to layer up in an attempt to harness the warmth of the body's core.

All of this comes at a rate and pace of its own, dictated by the constant cadence of the day, and governed by forces of nature older than time itself. With the brilliance of absolute silence my human condition slips out of time. Such a silence is beyond the negation of sound. It is a place of reality that I've come to enjoy. Suspended here, the world slows and brings me with it. For a moment or two a glimpse of diamond wisdom appears. It sprinkles a few nuggets of hope, bids me farewell, and then sends me on my way. Thank you old friend. With good fortune on my side, I'll return to visit on another day.

True to the words of John Muir: "In every walk with nature, one receives far more than he seeks." (16) We live in a beautiful place.

A Great Day for a Walk

I see a lot of wildlife as I make my way through the hills of Vermont and other places. For me, it's part of the allure that comes from nature. Often, the encounters are brief and photo opportunities are not always possible. Every now and again though, special moments occur and the gift of experiencing a prolonged visit with a majestic animal presents itself. I had one of those chance interactions today that lasted for 15 minutes or so. It might have lasted longer if I felt like hanging around more.

I first spotted the rack of this big fellow through the trees and about fifty yards away. He turned, made eye contact with me, and slowly started to move away as I took the first photo. I watched him work his way along a ledge while casually glancing back at me. I tried to quietly follow to keep my eyes on him. It didn't appear that I was too much of a concern for him as he unhurriedly moved up through the rocky terrain to a higher point on the ledge.

As I continued along the trail I passed beside and then around him taking a few pictures as I moved. He finally turned broadside and looked directly at me. At that point I was roughly 30-40 yards away. I took the final picture then and spoke out to him for a little while in an audible voice.

I let him know that he was majestic and a beautiful creature. I thanked him for sticking around and hanging out with me. Eventually I gave him a salute and decided to walk away. Before going around the ledge, I turned around again, and he was still there locked in a gaze with his eyes on me. I waved a final goodbye to this magnificent White-Tailed Buck and told him to be careful out there.

What a wonderful experience. We live in a beautiful place!

Peace in Gratitude

The familiar landscape of Smuggler's Notch is particularly appealing to me in the early winter. The road is closed, snow and ice secure their seasonal foothold, the ski areas have yet to open, and the pace of life slows. Especially true on a weekday morning, an air of serenity hangs suspended in time. On this bluebird November day, it was very peaceful.

So much so that I had the place to myself for the ascent. Of course, that meant breaking trail, but with about a foot of snow (with the exception of a few 2-3-foot-deep drifts) the going was pretty straightforward. Thus, I trudged along and did my best to absorb the abundant beauty. It was everywhere and it was soothing.

As Thanksgiving week is upon us, I couldn't help but wax poetic about the Grace in my life with a sense of gratitude in my heart. To be honest, it hasn't always been that way for me. Like many folks, I've suffered from my own set of self-centered miseries and too often lamented in a mud puddle of negative thoughts. In retrospect a necessary part of the process of life for each one of us and one for which I am grateful. The fact is, if I didn't live through that misery, I would still be living in it. Coming out on the other side is where growth has occurred. Nothing perfected mind you, but psychological, spiritual, and emotional, maturity has made its way. Often with me kicking and screaming in the wake, but progress has been made.

One of the many gifts that Grace has ushered into my life is awareness of that Grace. That awareness has helped me understand that it's fruitless to wait around for someone else to change your life. The stark reality is that the person that an individual waits for is the one looking back at them from the mirror. To be the person that you've been waiting for, live your life with purpose.

Trust that the Universal Grace that put you here did it for a good reason and that all of your life (good, bad, beautiful, and ugly) happens for your benefit. The truth is that this Universal Grace comes from a place of incomprehensible love. It's up to each one of us to live life in that love as we are that love. Because that's the only thing that we know for sure. That through every triumph, every failure, every fear, every act of courage, every loss, and every gain that a person experiences until the day one dies, comes through the reality of your life. Be present for it. This is not a rehearsal, it's your opportunity and yours alone.

Each time life is telling you that you are not good enough. That some person, place, or thing is the source of your problems. That you are broken or not worthy. Don't listen because that voice of doubt comes from a place of fear that is tucked away deeply within the ego self, and in its self-centered function, it will continually pull you away from your purpose. Have faith in the Grace that brought you here it knows the way. Pick yourself up, dust yourself off, and move through whatever it is that life has thrown your way. It might be difficult to move through and at times you might feel like it's too much. But persevere and believe in your worth. You came into the world from a place of Universal love and with a purpose. Trust the Grace that is the source of your creation and it will help you find joy in life that is beyond comprehension.

As I made my way through the mountains today beauty was abundant. It helped me appreciate the Grace, the love, and the good fortune of being right here right now. True love of life qualities working in a purposeful manner and through an interconnected Grace. The immensity of it all humbles me.

May each of you have a peaceful week of Thanksgiving and may moments of gratitude settle within. All the best.

Believe

I had the good fortune this week of spending a couple of enjoyable days hanging out with my grandson, Mason. Admittedly, the rate and pace of a four-year-old boy tires me out rather quickly. But it also gives me plenty of moments to learn, unlearn, and relearn deeper truths about life. The fact is, four-year-olds are brutally honest, kind and thoughtful too mind you, but brutally honest.

It seems that wisdom often finds its way to the surface more quickly when I get my 60 something self out of the way. Then listen and relearn things that I thought I already knew. God's Grace often shines brightest through the mind of a child. If only I can remember to nurture my own soul with that same childlike curiosity. Ever onward...

I had some time yesterday to take a long and quiet walk. In the process, as I often do, I let the last couple of days work through myself in contemplation. Not a practice that I've perfected, but a practice, nonetheless. The below theme resonated and it seems apropos for the month of December.

In the hustle and bustle of the season we sometimes lose sight of the reason for the season. For me, Jesus is the reason and the season. Some of you might appreciate my thoughts, some might find them indifferent, and others might find them downright offensive. So be it. I'm not judging anyone else's approach. It's none of my business what someone else thinks of me or my beliefs, that's their business. My business is to believe, to be honest, to be true with myself, and to be as selfless, kind, and thoughtful as I can be. Just like a four-year-old child.

What better time to express selfless actions than now? Regardless of what path anyone chooses to walk down, there is ample opportunity to add (or give) to the common good as we journey through the flow of life. As such, I offer the below and I wish each of you a peaceful and joyful Christmas season.

What is one of the most selfless things that you have done in life?

I have no idea. Sometimes I'm just the opposite. Totally wrapped up in a comfortable little bundle of selfishness and thinking about me, 24/7. "Every man must decide whether he will walk in the light of creative altruism or in the darkness of destructive selfishness." - Martin Luther King. (17)

As Dr. King alludes to, the darkness of selfishness and the light of creative altruism are choices that we all get to make. In my opinion, these choices present themselves to us often and have an effect on what path we take as we walk through life. If I start making determinations about how selfless my actions are, then I'm probably heading down the wrong path.

I was fortunate to have had some great role models in my life who exemplified selflessness through their actions. Without exception, the lack of fanfare was a common thread woven through each of these fine folks. In the course of their daily lives, altruistic acts came rather naturally. There was no drama, chaos, or confusion. No chest pumping, prideful boasts, or subtle hints made to shed light on themselves. In fact, most of the time we don't even know that an altruistic act was performed until sometime after the fact. It seems that truly generous folks conduct themselves this way. My hope is that on occasions I have somehow stumbled my way down the path set by these wonderful human beings, and performed some noble selfless acts. Lord knows, many times I have not.

Fortunately, each day is a chance to start over. Even throughout the day, opportunities continue to come along, and I get to choose how I respond. The best hope that I have of living in the light of creative altruism, is to maintain an awareness that there is a significance to my insignificance. Even though I am a small speck of dust in the cosmic flow, my actions matter, and because of that truth, I need to get my mindset oriented correctly at the start of each day. My self-centered Ego will not lead me down a path of selfless behavior. The grace of Divine Love (God) will give me a chance. Praying for direction, and then doing the next right thing, is about the best that I can do.

When I'm on point and full of conviction, opportunities to be a channel of God's peace present themselves. Being open-minded, honest about my place in the universe, and willing to receive Good Orderly Direction, then I am in a place where I can be of service to humanity. By the grace of God, sometimes I do ok.

The following poem offers some insight into selfless actions that add to the common good. The choices that we make matter. Perhaps we can all find opportunities throughout the days ahead to take actions with others in mind. Just think about the positive impact of that approach. All the best to each of you and Merry Christmas!

One Short Day
In this short day
Be an example of kindness
Walk with a heart of compassion
Endure the moments with patience
Broaden your mind with understanding
Embrace the strength of tolerance
Sow mutual respect
Be open to the warmth of grace
Shine your light on dark places
Spread hope to all you greet
This is your one day
Live it well
—Terry Lovelette, September 30, 2019

"You received without payment; give without payment." (Matthew 10:8)

The Heart of Nature

I love the winter and the first healthy snowfall. It brings back great memories of my childhood and the excitement of waking up to a fresh dumping of snow. Too many years have passed for me to recall exact moments in time. But I do recall gobbling down scrambled eggs and toast. Making a quick phone call or two to round up some neighborhood pals. Then hustling to layer up and get out into the joy of a winter wonderland where adventure ensued.

In those days, we layered up well in whatever woolen winter wear we could find. It didn't matter if a matching set of anything existed, and color coordination wasn't a concern. It only mattered that you had stuff to keep you warm. Often that meant wrapping your wool socked feet with bread wrappers to help keep the socks dry in your thinly insulated green rubber boots. The hope being that you could stay a little warmer and play outside a little longer. I enjoyed it then and I enjoy it now.

There's just something about it that gets me very close to the heart of nature. I find a great deal of beauty in the way the snow piles up and forms into artwork of a higher order. Consider the majestic reality that every individual flake comes with its own identity and joins with a collection of other unique creations in an interconnected embrace to present a remarkable landscape of beauty. If we give it a chance, not unlike the world we live in, IF, we give it a chance.

The backroads and wooded trails of Vermont bring a pleasing brand of winter scenery to the eye. If one takes a moment to pause you just might find yourself in a little piece of heaven. Right here, right now. In the stir-less silence a gentleness comes. It brings a message of serenity that soothes the soul and opens a gateway to a peace that goes beyond human understanding. If only we pause long enough to let that Grace work its everlasting way. It's there for all who do.

Have a peaceful day and rest in the moments with gratitude.

A Majestic Reality

It was a beautiful sunny day for a hike on the Winter Solstice. Conditions were perfect and temperatures were mild. Recent snowfall created a magical presence in the woods and the rime ice clinging to the trees offered the perfect complement. Sunlight bounced around inside it all quite remarkably making the entire experience pristine. Truly a walk through a winter wonderland.

Prior to my walk this morning I read an article that explained how long it takes light carrying photons from the sun to reach the surface of the earth.

Thanks to some really intelligent folks at phys.org who did the heavy lifting, I was able to glean a rudimentary understanding from some complex stuff.

It's always possible that I didn't get it right. However, my understanding is that photons are created by fusion reactions inside the Sun's core. They start off as gamma radiation and then are emitted and absorbed countless times in the Sun's radiative zone, wandering around inside the massive star before they finally reach the surface.

Amazingly, these photons that touched my eyeballs today were actually created tens of thousands of years ago and it took that long for them to be emitted by the sun. Once they escaped the surface, it then took only a short 8 minutes (or so) for those photons to cross the vast distance from the Sun to the Earth, work their majestic way, and help create the beautiful images that I was fortunate enough to see today. (18)

And this on the shortest day of the year. I'm routinely blown away by the majestic reality of the universe. All of which is held within an amazing amount of Grace. We live in a beautiful place.

An Inspired Life

Twenty Twenty-Two was my first full year of retirement. Within the year, I covered a little bit of ground and (hopefully) made some progress. Tiny steps over varied ground accumulated into 1350.5 miles of hiking last year.

Whether with family, friends, or just me and the Grace of my Higher Power, I enjoyed every step and I'm grateful for the many blessings in my life. I find hope and inspiration in nature. Frankly, taking the action to spend time outdoors makes more sense to me than indulging in the drama, chaos, and confusion that is so prevalent in our society today. Not that I ignore society. I just choose to not let the churn dictate how I view life. Instead, I walk around, look for inspiration in the beautiful place that we get to live in, write reflections on the messages that come my way, and openly share all of that here.

Why? Because it brings me joy and helps me stay more aware of the Grace that holds it all together. I also hope that in some small way these little thoughts and messages of inspiration help others too.

As it is I'm not getting any younger, but I'll do my level best to soldier on in 2023. Here's some hen scratching that's been bouncing around in my little cabbage over the last week. Hopefully, it makes sense to you and helps in some small way. At least, right now anyway, I think it does both for me…

All the best to you in the days to come – Terry

An Inspired Life

The clock ticks away
For the hero and the coward too
Life moves on

No amount of will can change it
The steady drip of time
It erodes even the sturdiest rock

How do we spend our days
In pursuit of imitation
Misguided missions
Mistaking the voice of others for one's own

Those who want a mask
Have to wear it

The reflection in the mirror
A blurred vision
An identity unknown
Unlearn the habit of being someone else
Lest you be nothing at all
Destiny lays low in the soul
In a patient place
Nurturing time
Awaiting the moment
Blossoming the innermost being
Strong roots sowed by the divine
Direction appears
Awareness of Grace
A pathway of Acceptance

Intuitive trust
Change ensues

The New Year dawns
A fresh horizon
Dreams of desires
Light a flicker of thought

What will it mean
In the dynamic forces
Of your life
If they don't become incarnate

The old whispers
Shout doubt
Doubling down
Choking out progress

Fall into darkness
If you must
Wallow in despair
To find inspiration

Or

Live anew
It's up to you

Shake the sloth
Release the fear
Feed the faith
Hope remains

Take a walk
On a wooded path
In a quiet place
With an open heart

A Presence waits
In a prayerful place
If you know
What you're looking for

Then

It sparks the inner light
Let it shine bright
In the miracle of you
Live an inspired life

Renewal

A fter a long stretch of gray days, I was looking forward to a walk-in sunshine today. I was not disappointed. Although a little snow would be nice, at least the air was crisp enough to make it feel like winter.

Sometimes the wilderness is all around you. I truly believe that, on this day, the wildlife was just as excited about a crisp sunny day as I was. I had the good fortune today of sharing some of the forest with a few deer, a gray fox, a few gray squirrels, wrens and chickadees, a pileated woodpecker, a raven, and a barred owl. I spoke with them all. The owl and the raven spoke back. I also got to enjoy walking through the woods with the warm embrace of the sun. It makes everything resonate with life, including the trees and the moss-covered rocks.

I'm fortunate that I get to experience moments like these where worlds blend and I get to realize that I am part of a much larger whole. In those moments it becomes apparent that one doesn't just get to appreciate nature, but that we are nature. When I'm able to move slowly and deliberately through the woods I'm welcomed in. With just a sliver of awareness it's possible to better sense the surroundings with an intuitive openness. With it, a pathway of renewal helps lift my spirit and enables me to engage fully in the ongoing relationship that exists in the quiet corners of the natural world. It all makes perfect sense to me and I enjoy it immensely.

We live in a beautiful place...

Peaceful Serenity

Having a sense of what's good for us and then, making time each day to engage in a little of it, is one of the greatest discoveries of human life. This simple practice helps enable what is emerging from the deeper well inside us. Slowly, it works to peel away the busyness of society. At first a trickle of inspiration appears. Followed often by a full flow of creativity, contentment, and Grace. A flow that can take us through every troubling thought or obstacle, that on the surface, might seem immovable. Ultimately it ushers in ample opportunities to reflect on life with gratitude. Then, it sends you on your way with a peaceful serenity. Enough, at least, to last the day. We live in a beautiful place.

This Day

I woke up this morning
Thinking about this precious gift
A chance today

To see the world
To breathe in the day
To listen to the earth
To think grateful thoughts
To enjoy
To love
To embrace the beauty
To be alive

I get that chance today

So much is beautiful
In nature
Another name for God
What do I notice

If I stay present
I witness abundant life

In the arms of outreaching trees
In the fresh winter smell
In the rays of sun
In the silence

In the cool breeze on my face
In the shadows strewn about the forest
In the low hum of ice forming on the lake below
In the eyes of a porcupine

Thank you for the wonders
For opening my senses
For helping me tune in
To your creation and beauty

For the gift of this day
Thank you

Raeya Rose

Raeya Rose divinely sent
Heavens gift moonbeams descent

Beauty made innocence within
From peace you come to the worldly din

Life greets you here at a hectic pace
You face it all with ephemeral Grace

A little coo angelic sound
Endearing warmth love abounds

Sweet baby girl in a family's nest
Shine your light forever blessed

A Natural Philosopher

Sherry and I had the pleasure of hiking with a natural philosopher yesterday. It became evident on the drive to the trailhead when I stopped my truck to move some scrap wood, full of nails, that was littering the road. Fortunately, I avoided the nails sticking out of the blocks of wood and was able to gather the dozen or so pieces off to the side of the road. Driving away Mason said, "You have a spare tire, right grandpa?" Affirming that I did, he went on to let us know how important it is to be prepared. Because, you never know…

I make no secret out of my love for the natural world and the Grace that comes with it. Life enriching qualities for me and soul nourishment that makes for a fulfilling journey. Of course, nothing is ever perfect, especially me. But, in my life, it all moves closer to the ideal in the Great Outdoors. There, the Grace of God speaks to me in unimaginable ways. Yesterday, I was reminded to walk slowly with a child, then listen to God's Grace. I'm thankful for that love. It brings meaning and hope to life.

My hope for everyone is that we pause long enough each day to let a little bit of Grace settle within. Then, grumble less, smile more, and spread some of your own light throughout your days. Walking around with an attitude of gratitude never hurt anyone. It helps me remember that there will continue to be mountains to climb, but to always be humble and kind. Today, is a good day to recall the lessons taught by our little philosopher. It's amazing how easy it is for adults to forget the basics.

Walking slowly with our grandchild helped remind me not to forget the simple truths and to always be prepared. Because, you never know… We live in a beautiful place.

Lessons from Maisie

One of the recurrent themes that we hear repeatedly from spiritual teachings is that there is a blindness in the world. Perhaps even an unwillingness to open our eyes and truly see. In the chase of life, it is easy to ignore the detail in the subtle beauty held within creation. When we ignore that detail, we become numb, desensitized, and our vision clouds.

In that state of unrest, all the trappings of a divisive society run rampant. The slow creep of angst works itself within. Clouding one's thoughts and limiting our choices to a subconscious mix of dualistic judgements. This is better than that, my side is better than your side, I am better than you. In the process of the ensuing calamity, we make choices, and a blindness sets in. Not realizing that our choices are what brings on this kind of blindness, we close our eyes and avoid seeing reality. The truth of our own self-induced pain, the yearning to have all the right answers and to be smarter than someone else, the indifference, the lack of fulfillment. All choices that will leave one feeling empty and alone. Truly a difficult place to be.

Amid the drama, chaos, and confusion brought on by the choice to engage in the divisive actions of society, we lose our sense of beauty and wonder. In essence, we become blind to the daily gifts of Grace that are offered to us at no cost. In our fight to be right we simply refuse to see. It is important to me that I pause regularly to ponder these thoughts. Where and when am I closing my eyes? What am I trying to avoid? What am I missing? Is there someone in my life who hungers to be seen and heard? Am I shutting off a source of wisdom by restricting who I listen to?

Too often, I fall into the messiness and miss out on the beauty that rests right before my eyes. The distractions can, and do, cloud my vision.

Walking around the backyard with my one-and-a-half-year-old granddaughter (Maisie) opens my eyes. I only must be present to listen and learn. Through the eyes of wonder this beautiful little girl teaches an old man. Each flower is an example of beauty meant to be enjoyed. Each insect has a lifeform filled with mystery and intrigue. An example of the diversity of the world that we live in and the wonders of creation. This channel of peace comes through the mystery of Grace. The joy in Maisie's face and the excitement in her voice tells me that we are in the middle of a gift. We just need to open our eyes and breathe it in.

With her verbal skills in the early phase of development, I am not entirely sure what she is telling me. But she is passing on to me important lessons that I sometimes forget about. The truth is, Maisie is closer to the mystery of creation than I am. Although I am attempting to interpret the messages that she is delivering, her joy is telling me to be open to the immensity of love that is freely given to each one of us. It is there all the time and for everyone to see, hear, smell, taste, and touch each day.

When I drop the distractions it all becomes more apparent, and my little granddaughter is then the perfect teacher. Open your eyes and see. Open your ears and hear. Open your heart and embrace. Open your soul and let it flow within. Then, some wonderous things happen. My mind becomes calm, my heart fills with love, and there is peace in my soul. The giddy laughter coming from this little cherub and the twinkle in her eyes was affirmation enough that grandpa was able to learn a few lessons today. Thank you, Maisie, for taking the time to remind me to always listen and learn. Yes, we live in a beautiful place.

Inner Joy

One of the many benefits of retirement is the gift of time. After a lifetime of chasing the day, one gets to slow down and appreciate the moments as they occur. Certainly not a startling revelation. Just recognition of a simple truth.

Spending the day outdoors with the little "Rose Bud" brings out an inner joy. She sets the pace and reminds me that happiness isn't something that you find or acquire. No, you just have to get the conditions right and then wait. Those conditions aren't complex. They just require that you pay attention. When I do, I'm able to catch the beauty in the little moments. That's the place where a sense of purpose and meaning emerge.

Raeya has a knack for cutting to the chase and keeping you engaged. She's delightfully inquisitive and not bashful about pushing on the edges of the answers that I provide to her frequent questions. She keeps me on my toes, and I enjoy the banter very much! So much to be grateful for. God's Grace always at work...

Shadows

The human world in a chase
Scattered opinions
Echo chambers of judgement
Impulsive madness
Stewing in a cauldron of irrational logic
A virus of the soul

Far from the bustling pace
Out there in the quiet woods
Sunshine bounces through the trees
A thousand shadows cast

Prismatic reflections sparkle in the snow
They dance to a joyful tune
Heard deeply within
A glorious beat
The reverberations of silence

Something wondrous works
A peaceful rhythm
It begins in the solitude
In the company of the forest

Wild places lend a cure
Slowly the noise abates
Serenity opens a gate
Equanimity fills the space
Authentic wisdom flows
Whispered softly
It brings the gift of Grace

Authentic Nature

Today was one of those days that just invites you in. So, I couldn't resist taking a walk in the mountains. A late winter day that's full of warmth and sunshine sets the conditions right to cater to a true source of enjoyment for me. Long ago, it became apparent that you should never lose sight of who you are. The world, and people in it, will have all sorts of ideas about what they think you should be. But no one else walks in your shoes. No one else can fully understand the depth of what another's true self is.

Once you understand this truth, lean into your authentic nature. If it means you walk slow and steady up a mountain, then don't race. If you enjoy depth, then don't get swept away by breadth. If you would like to pen a few thoughts about what comes your way in these quiet moments, pen them. Ultimately, being centered within is a prerequisite for anyone who desires to find purpose and meaning with the Grace that holds it all together.

I'm not always there, but when I do get the chance to be more aware, it becomes apparent that we live in a beautiful place and it's on full display all the time. It's up to each one of us to find a path forward that enables us to recognize that beauty and rest well in the silence with deep appreciation.

The Shag Bark Hickory

It's peaceful to take a walk in the woods during a snowstorm. Everything is hushed. Especially the flood of thoughts that usually flow through my brain. Instead, there's a restful solitude brought on by the beauty of the surroundings that I find myself in.

I spend a fair amount of time in forests that are canopied under an awning of old-growth trees. Some older than me by decades and others that have called a particular forest home for two or three centuries. Think of the life those old-growth trees have witnessed during the slow tick of their internal clocks. Weather and wars, celebration and sorrows, dread and dreams, all echoed through the forest by beating hearts of countless humans. Many of which are now long gone.

I often wonder what the trees might say if they could speak. Maybe, they would say nothing at all. Perhaps instead they would continue to release pheromones of truth into the silent woods. Patiently offering a perspective on divine Grace that us hurried little human bugs have a difficult time embracing. It's possible, I suppose, that trees do offer us some useful insight.

Insight from the Shag Bark Hickory

Slow down my dust-mote friend. Let the wisdom settle. Put down the club and stop fighting life. It's a battle that can't be won. Take a minute. Listen to the low rolling hum. Breath in the musky air. Let it refresh your thoughts. Look around. See the majestic beauty. It's everywhere. All the time. Better still, open up your heart. Feel the rhythm of the earth. If you do, then you might see it with the soul for the first time and witness the interconnected embrace that holds it all together. Go ahead, give it a shot. Your kind sure does whine a lot. All caught up in self-centered frights and urgencies. You might just find that when you stop thinking about yourself all the time, there's much more room for joy.

It was peaceful and beautiful out there in the woods today. I hope that you enjoy a little piece of it here. We live in a beautiful place!

Mysterious Grace

In the cold unrelenting bite of winter, it's hard to imagine spring. Colors of the landscape are resolved to tones of whites, blacks, greens, grays, and blues. All other hues seem to perish beneath the blanket of the season. Yet below the surface of winter the miracles of spring are preparing for their annual debut. As the angle of the sun crests atop the midpoint of the earth, the cold is relenting. The snow becomes saturated with a life-giving resource that slowly drips into the forest floor. Seeds held in repose are awakening to the steady flow of transition. Imperceptibly, one tiny spider crawls out from a place of hibernation, makes its way across patches of snow, then scours the mossy ledge for life giving sustenance. The symphony of renewal is no longer reversible. From the cloistered heart of winter, a miraculous opening is occurring. While the beauty of nature insists on taking its time, everything is prepared, and nothing is rushed. The rhythm of emergence in the gradual slow beat of the season is unfolding in perfect cadence. (19) With a mysterious Grace, that none of us really understand, nature's change remains faithful to itself. Soon, the snow will completely melt, the humus of the forest will convert the mud and muck with persistent confidence, and spring will fully bloom. Because nothing is abrupt in this seasonal flow, most of us will be caught unaware, the shades of spring will sprout gradually and one at a time. Even before we see it, breathing a plenitude of colors, the air will smell fresh. Then, we can look nowhere without seeing it. A marvelous renewal of life. Worthy of everyone's gratitude and deep appreciation. We live in a beautiful place!

An Arctic Chill

It's earth day 2020 as I head out for a morning walk
The wind blows cold out of the north at a steady 15mph
At 20 degrees (or so) Fahrenheit, it howls with an artic chill
I hesitate in my old pick-up truck listening to classic country on the radio
With the heater cranked high I'm quite comfortable
Mumbling words of a George Jones tune the trail head sign catches my eye
A subtle reminder that I'm here for a hike

With some trepidation I turn off the truck and open the door
Stepping into the elements allows the wind to find places to work itself inside my clothing
I zip up tighter to block out the openings

As I head out on the path words of despair ring through my mind
...You shouldn't be out here you fool
...You're too old for this crap, head south
As always, I ignore the voices and trudge along

Inspired by the biting wind my gait is steady and at a rate just outside of my comfort zone
A bead of perspiration forms on my forehead, soon a streak of cold works its way along my brow. Somehow, it all seems right

The trees speak a different language in the morning cold
Their moan is hardier and more robust
It almost sounds like they offer you a warning
...Feeble human, enter at your own risk
Elastic trunks bend and sway
Limb's crack and pop
Some lay on the trail
A reminder that nothing last forever
Rousing thoughts of my ultimate demise flood my brain
...Will it happen today?
...Maybe one of those limbs from the big oak tree has my name on it?
Subconscious banter can cast an unsettling darkness

The muse within me plays, poetic thoughts flow
An eagle soars over the ridge line
Within the backdrop of a snow-covered mountain, it presents a majestic image
Two pileated woodpeckers engage in a ritual flight of loops and dives
They ended on a nearby tree in a dance surely inspired by love
All the while in a full song of squawks, rattles, and piping calls
Gratitude eases me back to the moment and warms the soul
Nature's splendor is always at work

A Rainy-Day Walk

A rainy walk in the forest
Slows the pace of the day
When you move quietly within

Then
A gentle silence echoes
Like the mystics claimed

Felt in your heartbeat
In the rhythm of breath
A cathartic tempo

The old ones held it close
Wrapped in warmth
Nurtured with reverence

Listen to learn
Release the grip
Free cluttered thoughts

Watch them fly
Away they go
Carried by the wind

Dispersed to wide open spaces
Let them settle
Soon they'll root

Sprouting a vision
Provoking direction
Musings of inspiration

Conceived out of nowhere
Creative designs begin
A path to follow

From a stump
Reflections of life
Divine brilliance

Contours of time
Woven in mystery
A world of charm

Beauty abounds
Fashioned in spaces
A feast for the eyes

With equanimity
I admire your work
Awestruck by Grace

A puzzle for the mind
A place of rest for the heart
Grateful moments for the soul

Patience with the Day

Have patience with the day. By opening our eyes and casting a listening ear there stands a chance that one might stumble upon the grace of empathy as it floats through the woods. The Eastern Towhee and the Ovenbird seem to know. The Northern Cardinal and the Carolina Wren aren't shy with their opinions either. Letting me in on nature's secret. As Rilke suggested, "To love the questions more than the answers." (20) To be open to the mystery in the beauty and diversity held within the wisdom of the natural world. If I do, it speaks heart to heart in a language of beauty. With a dialect of complexities and a richness that leads you down the path.

In a slightly different way, all of us living things are on earth trying to survive the struggles, to be good at who we are, and to do good with some purpose. Within the spirit of reciprocity, we flourish. A bird is a bird, a flower is a flower, you are you, and I am me. Nothing can be anything other than what it is.

By living the questions now it's possible to find a meaningful pursuit that helps us play our greatest role. One where we stand a chance to form a deeper appreciation for life and the beauty held within the sundry of creation. Perhaps then, and sometime farther down the path, one might gradually start to notice that we are living our way into the answers of questions that we once loved. When you get there, love more questions, and live your way toward more answers.

We are all in this together and we live in a beautiful place…

Each Day

E ach day, and one day at a time, I start my day by saying Thank You. Why? Because it is important for me to start my day with an awareness to cultivate the spirit of gratitude. With it comes an underlying joy, as well as an appreciation for life. I am not boasting about this truth because it does not come from me.

Frankly, the more that I get out of the way, the better it gets. Letting go and letting God brings in a tranquil way. The mind becomes calmer, the heart holds more love, and peace rests in the soul. From that place of acceptance, I have a chance to focus on my own set of quirks and idiosyncrasies. The more effort that I apply to improving myself the more accepting I am of everyone else. I am fortunate today to be able to realize these truths.

Saint Augustine once said, "it will be solved in the walking." I tend to agree with that insight. Yet most of the time I am not always sure what it is that needs to be solved. Therein lies the mystery. The question then becomes, what intention do I walk with? If I walk in my own mind, I am restricted to the insight offered by the Ego. My experience has shown me that the ruminations of an egocentric walk can be distressing and will leave me in a state of unrest. With a slight shift in my intention, a walk in the mountains will energize both my mind and my spirit. The healing power of nature awakens my senses and offers new perspectives. When I move my body, I move my spirit as well. Taking this action in the outdoors connects me with the earth and affirms my own embodiment with the interconnected Grace that weaves through all of creation. Somehow, I am better when I walk with the intention of letting go and letting God. I find that mystery compelling.

As it is, the mountains lend a cure and offer an opportunity for some introspective thought. If I can get out of the way, then I have a chance to learn a little bit more about myself. Sometimes it happens quickly. But most often, it is a slow and gradual process. Regardless, like the roots of trees that work their way into the cracks of rocks to establish a strong foot hold, those meaningful insights work their way within me and become anchored. Then, without me even realizing it, my awareness increases, and new perspectives are formed. The whole process is beyond me, but I appreciate and accept it as a necessary part of my wellbeing.

In the middle of it all, you realize that when you pursue your passion you become graced with wonder. Then, it all starts to reveal itself in a purposeful way within the intricate detail of nature. The dullness of the world melts away and you get to experience the multitude of wonder that exists within everything. Always there and available to anyone who chooses to see.

So much of our experience depends on how we look at things and what actions we choose to take. My experience is that the quality of my looking determines what I allow myself to see. All that I need to do is accept the invitations that are freely sent my way. When I do accept them, the mystery and beauty of nature illuminates the world. The stuff that is never talked about stirs inside into a healthy blend of inner peace. An interconnected love, if you will, that holds it all together. It's everywhere, all the time, we only need to choose to see it and allow ourselves to be it.

To all of you; be kind to each other and follow your passion. Therein lies a purpose that comes with a meaningful Grace. No matter what the circumstances are in life, keep moving forward, the best is yet to come.

A Perennial Philosophy

What do we need most? Not for me to say. But as it is, I'll take a mountain day. A slow steady climb in silence just captivates me. Sun beams casting shadows through the sparse springtime canopy, it helps me find a way to sort out the busyness of life. Speaking a wordless language, a Perennial Philosophy whispers messages of profundity. They bring a peaceful calm. It's a good day to be alive and make a little progress. I'm grateful for this gracious gift.

With a slight shift in perspective, one can slowly move away from the mob. That lively hub of activity, full of discontent, and the breeding ground of angry rants. A home for many folks but no longer a place for me. Instead, I give myself plenty of quiet time. The silence of nature just welcomes you in. Offering steady reminders of who we are in the greater process of life. Humbling realities of our feeble existence in the cosmic order of time and space. The immensity of it all compelling and the mystery of the interconnected truths completely fascinating.

It helps focus the power of thought while reminding anyone who listens that the world is full of inspiration and on full display all of the time. Finding strength in meaning within the wonders of creation is ours for the asking. All we have to do is seek the truth and it will find us. Certainly, stepping into the unknown can sometimes be a little scary and it comes with risk. Yet, the non-risker doesn't grow, he just gets older. Stewing in a cauldron of toxic thoughts, his tongue speaks an unhealthy bitterness.

While I've traveled along that lonely path, I was offered seeds of growth. They started to sprout when I allowed them to be nurtured by Grace. As it is, each one of us is exactly where we need to be and we walk on fertile ground. Becoming as we become.

Presented to each of us in our own unique way, comes the power of choice. Those micro moments are breeding grounds of opportunity. Double down and fight to be right or find some inner peace by releasing the grip on the drama, chaos, and confusion brought on by one's own stubborn approach to life. I suppose it's easy to see this perspective unless it isn't. Yet once the mind opens up, the heart becomes willing, and the language of the soul waltzes in to clean up the mess. Only through this process of renewal can one start to see their own skin in the game. Once you choose this option it's possible to find a new freedom and a new happiness. It comes without much of a stir, and it helps anyone who listens understand that how we choose to live each day is how we choose to live our lives.

Like a flight of birds crossing your path, those old combative ideas fly into view and continue on their way. Free to litter the ground as they fall from your release. Like the farmers who fertilize with toxic manure, even these old poisonous thoughts can foster new growth. We still need to weed our garden by removing the roots of negative thoughts, but the seeds of positivity will grow deeper when we do. Those seeds will grow into a bountiful harvest.

I haven't invented any new truths, or offered any earth-shattering revelations, I just stumble upon them as I make my way. I can't see them when I'm wrapped up in my own self-centered point of view. So, I need to continue to get out of my own way. When I do, it's possible to contemplate the beauty that we get to live in. Always a source of strength and constantly flowing from a reservoir of inspiration. Enough to endure the struggles of life while offering an infinite amount of healing found in the everlasting arms of nature. It can keep one going as long as life lasts. Find a way to let it bring you some equanimity while you enjoy the moments of your day. We live in a beautiful place!

A World of Wonders

Every now and again, take a moment to step outside of yourself. To pay close attention to something small. When you do, it becomes mysterious, it can be seen more clearly, and with a fresh perspective.

A blade of grass, a pollinator in a source of nectar, a dandelion floret, or the brilliant structure of a pappus fiber and it's seed head connection. An indescribable world awaits. Each time we look, the deeper we peer. Ultimately, it starts to become clearer.

One layer opens up to the next and the next to another. Slowly peeling away the onion of discovery it appears. The spellbinding magnificence of nature. Beauty abounds.

Isn't this the way to look at the world? With the eyes of childlike wonder? Not as a collection of objects to be conquered but as gifts with hidden meaning? For me, a reasonable approach.

If we don't take that moment and rest in a peaceful pause. We miss the wonders right there at our feet. To appreciate the understory of the forest opens a portal of Grace.

It invites the soul to listen, and a reverent silence speaks. In the arms of creation, a gracious voice whispers. It resonates within and reminds us all to be still and to see the glory. A miraculous world of wonders awaits, and it brings a subtle joy to each day.

A Cascade of Water

As I was walking the other day, I came upon a cascade of water falling over a ledge. Nothing spectacular in the world of waterfalls, but a waterfall, nonetheless. Since this trail I was on has been around for over one hundred years it occurred to me that many others might have stood in this same spot to listen and observe as I did. For most of those years, and prior to the advent of our beloved electronic devices, folks got to stand there and simply take it in. So that's what I did.

As I stood there, the carousel of thoughts slowed to a whir. A minute or two later a slight hum. Then, just the sound of the little waterfalls mixed with birdsong and the cadence of a soft breeze rustling through the alpine forest. In a world in search of shocking events, this moment and place had nothing to offer. Instead, it just did what it does, and it was done with perfection.

For me, it's not necessary to quantify the healthful impact that these serene settings have on a person. Instead, I simply take it in with appreciation. An appreciation that my young brash self-had a difficult time with. Impatiently, that hurried soul chased life a little too much, and in the process, always had a need to break the silence. Heaven forbid you stay within that peaceful place because you might start getting acquainted with yourself. Nope, it seemed better to move, hurry, and chase. But as it is; no matter where you are, there you are.

On this day, I was standing in a beautiful remote location that was full of serenity. You won't find this place on an all-trails app or pinned as a selfie post on anyone's social media feed, not even mine. In the realm of jaw dropping beauty, this little spot isn't even on the list. But it's beauty in creation, nonetheless.

This simple practice of slowing down and being aware of the immense beauty that's all around us has taken a lifetime to learn. Silence in solitude brings on the holy. These moments are pure and full of the spirit. If you let it, it will draw you in and bring you peace. A peace that goes beyond my understanding. I don't have to hurry or chase; I just stand there in silence and let it embrace me. Sated, I moved along. Grateful and feeling content.

We live in a beautiful place...

The Greatest Poet

Sometimes as I begin my walk, it takes a few minutes to shake off the busyness of the day. When I wake up, the forest keeps its eyes on me. If I'm paying attention, wonder springs. The quality of my attention is directly correlated to my ability (or inability) to let go. On a good day, joyful moments grace the path.

With the smokey air from Canadian wildfires filtering the sun's rays, an orange glow is cast. Eerily, it piques my interest and heightens my focus. Slowly, an attentive gladness whispers the native poetry of the universe. Perhaps one of the purest forms of prayer, and maybe even, one of the truest glimpses of reality that exists.

Suddenly the trees fade into the forest and what you can't normally see appears. You begin to realize that the spirit of poetry is limited by the restrictions of the soul. The scope of the subject matter far beyond the shape and size of your surroundings. Within each breath is a lifetime and the understanding that we are all made of this. We are all blessed to be here living in the circle of motion called consciousness.

Will we wake up enough to see it? Will we take the chance and be it?

Many of the greatest things are accomplished in silence. Once we shed the need for noise and the display of grandiose emotions, a doorway opens. It offers a deeper clarity of inner vision and a quiet place of reflection. In that place, Grace works its way, the heart is quickened by love, and free will stirs us into action. That silent force brings the strength to endure the struggles. All one has to do is listen to the silence and let the greatest poet speak. Usually, the verse is simple and clear. Have faith in the wisdom of that truth.

The Gift

I get to call this place home
The beautiful Green Mountains

Somewhere higher up
A hermit thrush serenades the day

In such places the sacred sings
Revelations discovered simplistically

Sunbeams paint the forest
Illuminations of Grace in every ray

There's no way to help anyone understand
Though you wish they could

All the shoulds in the world make no difference
When a calloused heart shackles the brain

Many just don't have the capacity to go beyond
When the heart has turned to stone

Prayer and love are the only remedies
A subtle acceptance that can't be forced

My small adventures play over and again
Little fears that seemed big

All the material things that I had to get
A futile chase for fulfillment

The mountains teach the lessons
The only thing is to live

To learn to see the blessings
As the new day dawns

Let go of yesterday's sorrows
Rest well in the light that fills the world today

Be present for it
It is the gift...

Welcome Home

A t some point in time, it occurred to me. Poetry doesn't come from the inside out. It comes from the outside in, and then, it works itself out. Life is that way too. When you begin to see it all with that perspective more things make sense. You start to notice things in ways not considered before. In a universal cycle of reciprocity, those things will offer words and the words will offer things.

The world, and everything in it, emerges from your deep sleep. That little cocoon of isolation that some folks call the ego self, unabashedly steps aside. It kindly makes room for Grace. That Grace helps you understand that you are living with new conditions. Those conditions will help you understand the endless opportunities presented each day. In those opportunities are vital possibilities just lying there waiting to be discovered. Each one full of meaning and relevant in their apparent insignificance. Just like you and just like me.

Grace will let you see this more quickly. For a while things might seem slightly out of focus. It takes a moment to adjust the lenses. Yet, in its own time it happens. When it does, the significance of the insignificant becomes more obvious.

The interconnected web of life will embrace you in a natural flow of love. Not the obsessive kind talked about in the drama of things. But one that offers a peaceful insight and a fresh perspective. Connections will develop for you showing the linkages that exist. This is for that and that is for this. Petty thoughts melt away and creative ones appear. Presenting gifts at every turn, you see them in ways that you never did before.

They will shine their light on you, and you will be drawn to that light. In a wondrous form of gratitude, you will see the unexpected in the things you never paid attention to. Then you know what it is. You know that you have found your path, and you pursue that path with purpose. No longer is it about "look at me" it becomes all about "look at this!".

Nature will invite you in and fuel your feet with a righteous desire. The mountains will beckon and offer their praise. You will know when this is happening the first time you take a reverent pause; see things that you never saw before, breathe in the surroundings, and listen to the deep silence. In the quietude you will hear the whispers of truth that echo from the hidden wholeness. Welcome home young soul, welcome home!

Acknowledgments

"The beginning of our spiritual conversion is followed by a transition period that is always dark, confusing, and confining. Then comes a period of peace, enjoyment of a new inner freedom, the wonder of new insights. That takes time. Rarely is there a sudden movement to a new level of awareness that is permanent." —Thomas Keating.

As stated above, more will always be revealed. For each one of us and on our own spiritual timeline. Regardless, I hope that you have enjoyed reading some of my musings. I find that wisdom-based lessons are available everywhere and all the time. It is my belief that there is a spirit that permeates all of creation and serves as a great wisdom teacher. We simply need to be open to receiving the lessons that they teach and willing to learn, unlearn, and relearn deeper truths. An on-going process for me. My hope is that some of the insight passed on in this book inspires you to explore yourself and the beauty of the world that we live in. Both vessels of Grace and Blessings. Thank you!

The Author would like to express gratitude to all the kind folks (Family, Friends, and Acquaintances) who offered support, encouragement, and motivation toward the making of this book. Especially my Partner in Life Sherry King, for her love, friendship, patience, understanding, and belief in my vision. The mentorship and guidance from my publisher Ken Conklin and his wife Barbara. Two folks who define the word kindness. My Children, their spouses, and my grandchildren. Love, acceptance, and friendship personified in Grace. The vast fellowship of friends who offer support, acceptance, inspiration, and love. I am less without all of you. Somehow, and in some way, God made me a writer. He also Graced me with a love for nature and with an appreciation for the interconnected beauty that weaves through it all. His Grace has helped me find joy within each day and offers me a purposeful pathway to follow. I hike and write because I yearn to be closer to God. I offer this book as a form of gratitude.

I read regularly and I enjoy the insights offered by Thomas Keating, Thomas Merton, Anthony DeMello, Richard Rohr, Jake Owensby, The Bible, Pema Chodron, Mark Roberts, Thich Nhat Hahn, Ursala LeGuin, Lao Tzu-The Tao, Kahlil Gibran, C.S. Lewis, The Dalai Lama, Joy Harjo, The White Bison, Parker Palmer, Mary Oliver, Bill McKibben, Jack Kerouac, Maria Popova, Bertrand Russell, Bill Wilson, Tony Whedon, Henry David Thoreau, Ralph Waldo Emerson, Walt Whitman, John Burroughs, John Muir, John O'Donohue, Kent Nerburn, Jim Findlay, Chris Highland, Miller Williams, Gary Snyder, Jeffers, Rumi, Tagore, and many others. I also enjoy insights provided by the average Jane's & Joe's as well. Differing points of view help teach me, and orient me, as I walk around the subject of life and the world that we all live in. Thank you for your wisdom and thoughtful insight.

Notes

Introduction
    (1) John O'Donohue *Eternal Echoes: Celtic Reflections on Our Yearning to Belong*. Harper Collins, 2009, page 102

A Perspective
    (2) Epictetus. *The Golden Sayings. pXV*. classics.mit.edu/Epictetus/goldsay.1.1.html

In Memory of Henry David
    (3) Greenblatt, Lilly. Look Up. Lions Roar 17 May 2019. www.lionsroar.com/look-up/

Solitude in The Notch
    (4) Owensby, Jake. Struggling With The Truth. Jakeowensby.com. 19 November 2021. jakeowensby.com/2021/11/19/struggling-with-the-truth/

Quiet Places
    (5) Scalia, Elizabeth. The Power of the message: "It is good that you exist". Patheos 14 January 2015. www.patheos.com/blogs/theanchoress/2015/01/14/the-power-of-the-message-it-is-good-that-you-exist/

Cocoon of Thought
    (6) Piver, Susan. 5 ways not to bite the Trump Hook – Lions Roar. 16 February 2017. 5 Ways Not to Bite the Trump Hook - Lions Roar www.lionsroar.com/susan-piver-election-response/

    (7) Anelo, Megan. 16 Unforgettable Things Maya Angelou Wrote and Said. 28 May 2014. Maya Angelou Quotes: 16 Unforgettable Things She Wrote and Said | Glamour www.glamour.com/story/maya-angelou-quotes

Deeper Thoughts from A Walk

(8) Popova, Maria. 30 December 2016. John Steinbeck on Good and Evil, the Necessary Contradictions of the Human Nature, and Our Grounds for Lucid Hope. www.brainpickings.org/2016/12/30/john-steinbeck-new-year/ www.themarginalian.org/2016/12/30/john-steinbeck-new-year/

The Gift of Reciprocity

(9) Danzis, David. 22 January 2018. Candle Magick for Beginners. www.njherald.com/20180122/get-your-senses-going-at-the-magickal-pathways-in-newton?template=art_print

A Walk with the Birds

(10) Arnold, Colleen. 14 May 2022. Pause and Pray God Is Truly Right. www.franciscanmedia.org/pausepray/god-is-truly-right

(11) Pandya, Mamata. 31 December 2019. Looking Ahead. millennialmatriarchs.com/tag/herman-hesse/

(12) Bates, Sallye. 12 April 2015. A New Day. www.justapinch.com/groups/discuss/137261/4-12-a-new-day

A Hidden Field

(13) Quote by Anthony de Mello: "How does one cope with evil? Not by fighting it…" (goodreads.com)

It's Always There

(14) Smith, Huston. Why Religion Matters: The Fate of the Human Spirit in an Age of Disbelief. www.goodreads.com/author/quotes/6734.Huston_Smith?page=2

A Hidden Wholeness

(15) Thomas Merton *Witness to Freedom The Letters of Thomas Merton in Times of Crisis*. Farrar, Straus and Giroux 1995 reprint (public library)

An Old Friend

(16) Muir, John. Mormon Lilies, San Francisco Daily Evening Bulletin (part 4 of the 4 part series "Notes from Utah) dated July 1877, published 19 July 1877; reprinted in *Steep Trails* 1918, chapter 9. En.wikiquote.org/wiki/John_Muir

Believe

(17) Martin Luther King Jr. quoted in Michael Lynberg (2001). *Make Each Day Your Masterpiece: Practical Wisdom for Living an Exceptional Life. Andrews McMeel Publishing. P. 181.* en.wikiquote.org/wiki/Good-will

A Majestic Reality

(18) Cain, Fraser. 15 April 2013. How long does it take sunlight to reach the Earth? phys.org/news/2013-04-sunlight-earth.html

Mysterious Grace

(19) John O'Donohue *To Bless the Space Between Us.* The Crown Publishing Group. 2008. P. 47 www.goodreads.com/work/quotes/1199882-to-bless-the-space-between-us-a-book-of-invocations-and-blessings

Patience With the Day

(20) Rainer Maria Rilke translated by Stephen Mitchell, Edited by Ray Soulard Jr. *Letters to a Young Poet.* Burning Man Books is a Special Projects Division 201 Imprint of Scriptor Press. P. 13 Letters to a young poet p13 kbachuntitled.files.wordpress.com/2013/04/rainer-maria-rilke-letters-to-a-young-poet.pdf

Author Bio

Terry Lovelette was raised in Sheldon Springs, Vt. and currently lives in Saint Albans, Vt. He loves the rolling hills of the Green Mountain State and holds them dear with a sense of loyalty. He is a graduate of Johnson State College. He is retired from a 44-year career in the semiconductor industry. He spent 21 years as a volunteer Assistant Coach for the University of Vermont's Men's Ice Hockey team. He also enjoyed volunteering his time as a USA Hockey Coaching Director in Vermont, as well as a volunteer coach for various youth sports teams. As a passionate outdoor enthusiast, he enjoys an interconnected relationship with nature. His passion has helped fuel a love for hiking. He has walked over 1,000 miles yearly in the last decade and a half. Included in those journeys are through hikes of the Long Trail, The John Muir Trail, the Teton Crest Trail, and various other pathways in desert and mountainous areas of the US and Canada. His writings reflect the inspiration that comes from these journeys in a purposeful way.

Printed in the USA
CPSIA information can be obtained
at www.ICGtesting.com
LVHW061535280124
770160LV00050B/2564